北京的世界文化遗产
The World Cultural Heritage in Beijing

天坛

THE TEMPLE OF HEAVEN

姚安　王桂荃 编著

北京美术摄影出版社
BEIJING ARTS AND PHOTOGRAPHY PUBLISHING HOUSE

天坛全图
An Over View of the Temple of Heaven

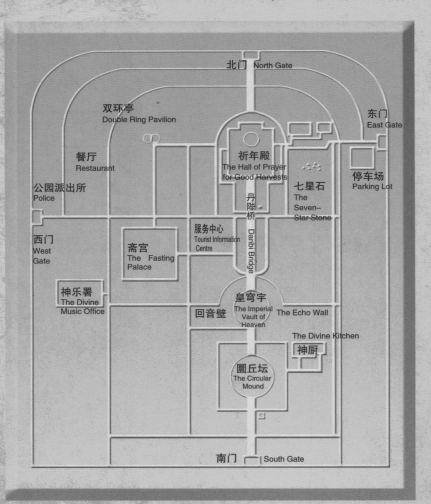

北门 North Gate

双环亭
Double Ring Pavilion

东门
East Gate

餐厅
Restaurant

祈年殿
The Hall of Prayer
for Good Harvests

公园派出所
Police

七星石
The
Seven–
Star Stone

停车场
Parking Lot

丹陛桥

服务中心
Tourist Information
Centre

西门
West
Gate

斋宫
The Fasting
Palace

Danbi Bridge

神乐署
The Divine
Music Office

皇穹宇
The Imperial
Vault of
Heaven

回音壁   The Echo Wall

The Divine Kitchen

神厨

圜丘坛
The Circular
Mound

南门
South Gate

天 坛

中国·北京市

列入日期：1998

符合准则：C (i) (ii) (iii)

The Temple of Heaven
Tiantan Park, Beijing
Date of Inscription: 1998
Criteria: C (i) (ii) (iii)

天坛建于公元15世纪上半叶,坐落在皇家园林当中,四周古松环抱,是保存完好的坛庙建筑群。无论在整体布局还是单一建筑上,都反映出天地之间的关系,而这一关系在中国古代宇宙观中占据着核心位置。同时,这些建筑还体现出帝王将相在这一关系中所起的独特作用。

The Temple of Heaven, founded in the first half of the 15th century, is a dignified complex of fine cult buildings set in gardens and surrounded by historic pine woods. In its overall layout and that of its individual buildings, it symbolizes the relationship between earth and heaven–the human world and God's world–which stands at the heart of Chinese cosmogony, and also the special role played by the emperors within that relationship.

目录 CONTENTS

一、礼乐自天子出
——神坛故事

A Story of the Divine Altar

宏伟壮丽的祈年殿 *The Magnificent and Splendid Hall of Prayer for Good Harvests*

　　在北京城正阳门东南,有一处面积广阔的古老园林。从空中俯瞰,在北圆南方的区域内,一条石堤大道纵贯南北,南有洁白如玉的祭天台,北有蓝瓦金顶的圆形大殿,路西则是精巧别致的方形殿宇。在万千松柏的掩映中,白色雕栏、蓝色琉璃、金色宝顶,以及圆形、方形、矩形各式建筑构成了一幅美妙的图画。人们置身其中,仿佛被包容、被感召、被溶化,变得渺小而微不足道,因而渴望获得升华。这座独具魅力的园林便是世界上最大的祭天建筑群——天坛。

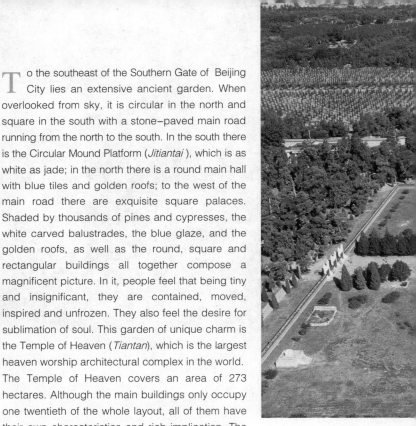

To the southeast of the Southern Gate of Beijing City lies an extensive ancient garden. When overlooked from sky, it is circular in the north and square in the south with a stone-paved main road running from the north to the south. In the south there is the Circular Mound Platform (*Jitiantai*), which is as white as jade; in the north there is a round main hall with blue tiles and golden roofs; to the west of the main road there are exquisite square palaces. Shaded by thousands of pines and cypresses, the white carved balustrades, the blue glaze, and the golden roofs, as well as the round, square and rectangular buildings all together compose a magnificent picture. In it, people feel that being tiny and insignificant, they are contained, moved, inspired and unfrozen. They also feel the desire for sublimation of soul. This garden of unique charm is the Temple of Heaven (*Tiantan*), which is the largest heaven worship architectural complex in the world.

The Temple of Heaven covers an area of 273 hectares. Although the main buildings only occupy one twentieth of the whole layout, all of them have their own characteristics and rich implication. The Temple of Heaven is built in the eighteenth year during the reign of Emperor Yongle of Ming dynasty, which is in 1420. It is the sacred altar for emperors of Ming and Qing dynasties to offer sacrifices to Heaven and pray for a bumper harvest. It has a history of 580 years. Ancient beliefs like "circular sky, square earth", "supernal heaven, low earth", and "blue heaven, yellow earth" are all exquisitely and ingeniously reflected here.

　　天坛占地273公顷，主要建筑只占整体布局的1/20，且各具特色，极富象征含义。天坛建成于明永乐十八年(1420年)，是明清帝王祭天祈谷的神坛，距今已有580余年的历史，"天圆地方"、"天高地低"、"天玄地黄"等观念在这里无不体现得精妙绝伦。

　　明永乐十八年(1420年)，北京天地坛按南京旧制建成，坛域南方北圆，主体建筑大祀殿，垣墙内西南建有斋宫。明嘉靖九年(1530年)天地分祀，大祀殿南增建圜丘台专用祭天，圜丘坛以北建有神版殿(原名泰神殿，后改名为皇穹宇)，形成南

明代皇穹宇
The Imperial Vault of Heaven in Ming Dynasty

In the eighteenth year during the reign of Emperor Yongle of Ming dynasty (in 1420), the Temple of Heaven and Earth was built in accordance with the old practices in Nanjing. The boundary of the temple was square in the south and circular in the north. The main buildings were the Great Hall for Sacrificial Rituals (*Dasidian*) and the Fasting Palace (*Zhaigong*), which were built in the southwest inside the walls. In the ninth year during the reign of Emperor Jiajing of Ming dynasty (in 1530), people offered sacrifices to Heaven and Earth separately, so the Circular Mound Altar (*Yuanqiu*) was built to the south of the Great Hall for Sacrificial Rituals and used only for Heaven worship. The Hall of Memorial Tablets (*Shenbandian*) was built to the north of the Circular Mound Altar and later it was renamed as the Imperial Vault of Heaven (*Huangqiongyu*). Thus the layout took shape that the Altar in the south and the Altar in the north were both located at the axis. In the 21st year during the reign of Emperor Jiajing (in 1542), the Great Hall for Sacrificial Rituals was demolished, and in the 24th year during the reign of Emperor Jiajing (in 1545) Great Hall for Offering Sacrifices (*Daxiangdian*) was built at this site. Great Hall for Offering Sacrifices was round and characterized by a cone-shaped structure with triple eaves. The base of the hall was a triple tiered marble terrace. Other major buildings besides the Circular Mound Altar were also round in shape and symmetrical from

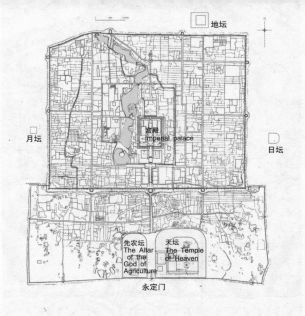

天坛与先农坛夹天街对峙
The Temple of Heaven and the Altar of the God of Agriculture Stand Facing Each Other with the Heavenly Thoroughfare in Between

北两坛依轴线布置的格局。嘉靖二十一年(1542年)大祀殿被拆除,嘉靖二十四年(1545年)在原址上建成大享殿,殿为圆形三重檐攒尖建筑,坐落在三层石台之上。同圜丘台对应形成主体建筑均为圆形并南北对称分布的格局,中间有圆形围墙包围着的重檐圆形建筑皇穹宇作为过渡,北高南低,由长达360米的丹陛桥将两坛联接形成统一的整体。

　　嘉靖三十二年(1553年),北京城南外城扩建,原南郊天坛被扩在北京城内。北京城中轴线南端为永定门,天坛位于外城永定门内即北京城中轴线南段以东,以西为先农坛。为壮观瞻,使两坛坛墙更加完善,同时也与整个北京城规划布局相谐调,天坛增筑外坛墙。形成天坛、先农坛两坛夹天街对峙,蔚为壮观的布局。天坛外坛墙建成后,仅西向设门,坛域扩大为273公顷。但连接南北两坛的轴线不居中,而位于中线偏东位置,打破了传统的主要建筑位于中轴线上的做法。这与整个北京城西城略大,东城略小的特点相一致。轴线偏东丝毫未使天坛建筑布局受损,

north to south in its layout. The Imperial Vault of Heaven was the transitional building in the middle, which was a round building with double eaves surrounded by enclosing walls. The buildings in the north were higher than the ones in the south and the two Altars were connected by Red Stairway Bridge (*Danbi Bridge*), which was 360 meters long, and by which the two parts were integrated as a whole.

In the 32nd year during the reign of Emperor Jiajing (in 1553), the south outer city of Beijing City was extended, so the former southern suburbs, where the Temple of Heaven was located, was included into the inner Beijing City. The southern end of the axis of Beijing City was YongdingGate and the Temple of Heaven was located at inner YongdingGate, which was to the east of the southern axis of Beijing City. To the west of the southern axis was the Altar of the God of Agriculture (*Xiannongtan*). To make a better sight, to improve the appearance of the two Altars, and to make the whole layout of Beijing City more harmonious, external walls were built outside of the Temple of Heaven. Thus the layout took shape that the Temple of Heaven and the Altar of the God of Agriculture stood facing each other with the Heavenly Thoroughfare (*Tiantan*) in between, which presented a splendid sight. After the building of the external walls, the Western Heavenly Gate was built as the

清初圜丘坛图,右下方建筑为崇雩坛,乾隆十二年(1747年)拆除
A View of the Circular Mound during Early Qing Dynasty. Chongyue Altar, the Building on the Lower Right, Was Demolished in the 12th Year during the Reign of Emperor Qianlong(1747)

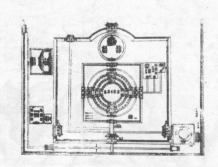

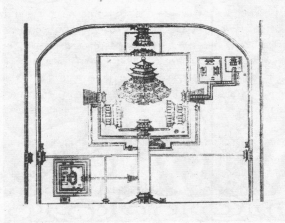

清顺、康、雍时代祈谷坛图
A View of the Altar of Prayer for Good Harvests during the
Reign of Emperor Shunzhi, Kangxi and Yongzheng

反而使得由西向东进入天坛的人更觉得坛域深远广阔。

清乾隆年间,天坛建筑进行了大规模扩建、改建及修缮。乾隆十四年(1749年)扩建圜丘坛,改建皇穹宇,将"大享殿"改名为祈年殿,并将大享殿三色瓦统一为青色,使得天坛建筑更加圣洁崇高,色彩鲜明浓烈,象征寓意更加丰富。乾隆十九年(1754年),在天坛西门外垣之南建门一座,称"圜丘坛门",原来的西门称之为"祈谷坛门",形成了天坛南北两坛单独成制、规制严谨的格局。至此,天坛建筑格局及建筑形式最终形成并一直保留到了今天。

当年的皇帝从紫禁城出发,走正阳门大街向南,过天桥,穿过繁华的闹市街区,向东便进入幽静深远的神坛禁地,开始他祭天的仪式。岁月流逝,时光带走了帝王的辉煌与荣耀,却留下了一座世界瞩目的美好园林。让我们沿着当年祭天的道路,进入天坛吧。

only gate of the Temple of Heaven, which made the area of the temple expand into 273 hectares. However, it also made the axis connecting the north and south altars being east of center rather than in the center, which was not in accordance with the traditional practice that the main building should be located at the axis. This situation was consistent with Beijing City's layout that the western district was a little larger than the eastern district. Therefore, that the axis was eastern of center didn't harm the Temple of Heaven's layout and on the contrary it made people entering the temple through the west gate see an even wider field and feel even greater reverence.

During the reign of Emperor Qianlong, the Temple of Heaven was extended, reconstructed, and repaired in a large scale. In the 14th year (in 1749) the Circular Mound Altar was extended, the Imperial Vault of Heaven was reconstructed, Great Hall for Offering Sacrifices was renamed as the Hall of Prayer for Good Harvests (*Qiniandian*), and its triple-colored tiles were changed to be unified grey tiles. These changes made the Temple of Heaven even more holy and pure, more sublime, more vivid and strong in color, and of more symbolic meanings. In the 19th year (in 1754), another gate was built to the south of the outer walls of the West Gate, which was called "date of Circular Mound Altar" (*Huanqiutanmen*), and the former West Gate was called "Gate of Altar of Prayer for Grain" (*Qigutanmen*). Thus the layout took the form that the north and the south altars were located separately with well-designed sizes, shapes and styles. The layout and style of the Temple of Heaven finally took shape then and have been maintained till today.

In those years, the emperors set out from the Forbidden City, went southward through the Southern Gate Street, crossed the platform bridge, walked along the bustling streets, Walking eastward, one will enter the tranquil and profound restricted area, and started the rites of heaven worship. Time went on and brought away the emperors' glory and honor. However, this splendid garden still stands here, which has attracted worldwide attention. Now let's walk along the path of heaven worship in old days and go into the Temple of Heaven.

In Qing dynasty every time before a stately heaven worship ceremony, the emperor would go out from the Forbidden City to the Temple of Heaven under heavy escort of the most spirited and imposing imperial guard of honor. In the forefront went guide elephants and treasured elephants. Wrapped with blue saddlecloth and with no

从双环亭眺望祈年殿

Overlooking the Hall of Prayer for Good Harvests from Double Ring Pavilion

other decorations, guide elephants looked mighty and splendid. Treasured elephants closely followed guide elephants, and they carried treasured bottles on their exquisite saddles, which implied the meaning of "Taiping You Xiang" (there are signs of peace and tranquility). Followed treasured elephants are Minwei (ancient official title of civilian minister in charge of military affairs) with whistling whips in their hands. After them was the grand music team. Most musical instruments were drums and pipes. Then it was the massive array of five chariots. The armed escort with *Yinzhang* and *Yuzhang* such arms followed with flags, banners, military big square banners, command flags and banners, cloaks, long narrow flags, pennants, streamers, umbrellas and canopies used in ancient Chinese honor guard. Baldachin, brocade, and tapestry satin made the scene even more colorful and spectacular. The most important part of the array went after the imperial bodyguards with weapons in hands. The eight gold pieces of things used by the emperor were carried first in the array. After that it was the nine-dragon crank yellow canopy,

大驾卤簿图局部——宝象，又称"太平有象"
A Part of the View of the Imperial Guard of Honor –Treasured Elephants, Which Is Also Called "Tai Ping You Xiang"

　　清王朝举行最盛大的祭天典礼前，皇帝在最气派、最炫耀的皇家仪仗队——大驾卤簿的簇拥下，从紫禁城前往天坛。走在最前列的是导象和宝象，导象身披蓝屉，不加羁饰，威武壮观。紧随的宝象，精美的象鞍上安载宝瓶，寓意"太平有象"。宝象后是手执静鞭的民尉。后有前部大乐的队伍，乐器多为鼓吹乐。接着便是五辂，声势浩大。随后便是手持引仗、御仗等兵器的队伍，旗、帜、纛、麾、氅、节、旌、幡、幢、伞、盖如云，织锦云缎，色彩斑斓。手举兵刃的亲军、护军出现后，整个队伍进入高潮。在皇帝使用了金八件后，是最能代表帝王威仪的九龙曲柄黄华盖。其后是皇帝乘坐的玉辇——36人抬的大轿，从紫禁城到天坛仅抬轿的备班就有十几班，数百人。簇拥皇帝的有前引大臣（均为二品以上官员），后有拿豹尾枪、挂佩刀及带弓矢的侍卫，文武百官、太监队伍，侍卫、护军等紧紧跟随，黄龙大纛压后，百官马匹在队伍最后相随，整个队伍绵延数里，浩浩荡荡。

大驾卤簿图局部——皇帝玉辇 *A Part of the View of the Imperial Guard of Honor—Yunian*

大驾卤簿图局部——皇帝礼舆 *A Part of the View of the Imperial Guard of Honor—Liyu*

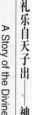
which symbolized the emperor's impressive and dignified manner. Then it was the imperial jade carriage (*yunian*), which was a huge sedan carried by 36 people. There were hundreds of people on call for carrying sedans by turns. The people gathering around the emperor were guide ministers (whose official ranks were higher than grade–two) in the front and the imperial bodyguards with spears of the form of marten tail in hands and swords or sabers worn at the waist, civil officials and officers of the armed services, eunuchs, bodyguards, guard army behind the emperor. After them there were big army banners with the design of yellow dragons. Then the horses of civil officials and officers ran at the end of the array. The whole array was quite grand and stretched for several *li* (1 *li* equals 1/2 kilometer).

If the emperor wanted to worship Heaven at the time of the winter solstice or offer sacrifices and pray for rain in the first month of summer, the array would enter through the Gate of Circular Mound Altar (today the front gate of the Hospital of Temple of Heaven, right facing the Altar of the God of Agriculture). If the emperor wanted to offer sacrifices and pray for a good harvest in the first month of spring, the array would enter through the Gate of Altar for Grain Prayers (today the West Gate of the Temple of Heaven).

If you walk eastward from the Gate of Altar of Prayer for Good Harvests, you will see a straight road stretching toward the depth of the ancient altar with dense trees on both sides and the Second Altar Gate (*Erdaotanmen*) standing majestically in the distance, and you will have the feeling of being cut off from the outside noisy world. After walking 450 meters toward east, you will come to the second altar gate, namely the Inner West Heaven Gate (*Nei Xitianmen*). Through the west second gate you will come to the inner altar area. All the buildings except Devine Music Office (*Shenyueshu*) are located in the inner altar area.

祈谷道路两旁的国槐树茂密、葱郁
The Luxuriant and Verdant Cypresses along the Roadsides of the Temple of Heaven

如果举行冬至祭天、孟夏常雩礼，队伍就入圜丘坛门（今天坛医院前大门，正对先农坛）；若举行孟春祈谷礼，则走祈谷坛门（今天坛公园西门）。

进入祈谷坛门东行，两侧树木茂密，一条笔直大道通向古坛深处，可看到远处二道坛门巍峨耸立，顿时有与尘世喧嚣隔绝的感受。东行约450米，来到二道坛门前，即内西天门。进入西二门后，便进入内坛区域，天坛建筑中除了神乐署在外坛，其余建筑都在内坛。

二、玲珑皇宫——斋宫

Exquisite Mini Palace: the Fasting Palace

斋宫东门
The East Gate of the Fasting Palace

　　斋宫在内坛西部,坐西朝东,是祭天大典前皇帝斋戒的宫殿。殿瓦采用绿色,以此代表皇帝对天称臣。每次祭祀前皇帝要到斋宫斋宿。

　　斋宫四周建有两重方形围墙,两道深池沿墙环绕,外围墙建回廊163间,是驻守重兵的地方,当年皇帝在此下寝,森严戒备,可见一斑。斋宫东向及南北向设拱券式宫门,门外是汉白玉拱桥架于御河之上,整座斋宫占地4万平方米,人称"小皇宫"。

　　从斋宫东门进入,北侧有钟楼,当年皇帝临坛行礼时,钟楼即开始鸣钟,警告官

俯瞰"小皇宫"——斋宫
Overlooking the "Mini Palace"— the Fasting Palace

明永乐大钟
The Bell Made During the Reign of Emperor Yongle of Ming Dynasty

无梁殿月台前的栏板、望柱及出水
The Balustrades, Columns and Chushui in Front of the Platform of the Hall without Beams

The Fasting Palace is located in the west of the inner altar area and faces east. It is the palace for the emperor to fast before the great ceremony of heaven worship. The glazes of the hall are green, which means that the emperor swears fealty to Heaven. Before the day of prayer, the emperor needs to live and fast in the Fasting Palace.

There are two layers of square walls and two deep pools around the Fasting Palace, and there are 163 winding corridors along the outer walls, where large number of troops garrisoned in those years. We can see how heavily the hall was guarded when the emperor lived here. There are arch gates in the east, south, and north of the palace and outside the gates are white marble arch bridges over the imperial river. The whole covers an area of 40,000 square meters and people also call it "mini palace".

Enter the Fasting Palace from its East Gate, you will see the Belfry on the northern side. In those years when the emperor came to the altar to worship Heaven, the bell rang to warn each official to perform his function. The bell was made during the reign of Emperor Yongle of Ming dynasty and its voice was resonant. Today visitors can still climb up the Belfry and knock the bell. On the southern side of the paved path leading to the hall there is another bell in the open air. This bell is made with superb craft and its figure is exceptionally beautiful. The lifelike inscriptions on it read "Made During the Reign of Emperor Qianlong" It is said that in the past the invaders took a fancy to this bell, and wanted to take it back to their hometown. They offloaded it from the Belfry, however, the bell was too heavy to carry, so they had to abandon it here. Today visitors may only see it stand quietly on the grass while they may not know how many vicissitudes it has experienced.

斋宫钟楼
The Belfry of the Fasting Palace

员各司其职。大钟为明永乐年间制造,声音洪亮,今人登钟楼亦可敲钟。甬路南侧露天有一大钟,工艺讲究,外形漂亮异常,上有款识"乾隆年造",蒲牢为钮,栩栩如生。传说当年侵略者看上了这座精美大钟,从钟楼上卸下,欲掠走他乡,终因太过沉重,不便携带而放弃。今人观其默默立于草地之上,岂知它经过多少沧桑。

清乾隆大钟
The Bell Made During the Reign of Emperor Qianlong of Qing Dynasty

铜人, 传为明朝乐官冷谦
The Bronze Figurine,
Which Is Said to
Be Devised by Lengqian,
A Musician Official in
Ming Dynasty

Through the Second East Gate people will enter **the central hall,** which is the main hall of the Fasting Palace. Since this hall is entirely made of bricks and tiles, it also gets the name of "Hall without Beams" (*Wuliangdian*). There are five rooms in this hall with green glazed arched tiles covering the hip roofs. The room whose door opens directly onto the courtyard is the place where the emperor met ministers during fast. In the middle of the room is the emperor's throne. After the throne there is a wood–folding screen, which is engraved with the design of landscape. Above the throne hangs a board inscribed "*Qin Ruo Hao Tian*" (Emperor is like the Heaven). The other rooms are for the ministers to rest and wait for the moment of heaven worship.

On the left side of the red steps leading up to the main hall is **the Pavilion of Fasting Bronze Figurine** (*Tongrenting*). The pavilion is made of stone with the height of over one zhang (one *zhang* equals 10/3 meters). Inside it there is a marble base. When the emperor came to the Fasting Palace to perform a fast, a bronze figure (about 40 to 50 centimeters high) with a fast tablet in its hand would be placed inside the pavilion so as to remind the emperor of observing fast commandments.

On the left side of the red steps is **the Time Pavilion** (*Shichenting*). The time to offer sacrifices and pray for good harvests was seven quarters before the sunrise, which was about the time of a quarter past four in the morning. At that time the officials of Tai Chang Si and Qin Tian Jian would send the time memorial to the throne to the pavilion, and then it was fetched out by the head eunuch to report to the emperor. Then the emperor would set out to get to the altar to perform the heaven worship rites.

Behind the main hall is the hall where the emperors sleep.

太平水缸 *Taipingshuigang* (A Bronze Vat Used to Put out Fire)

无梁殿
The Hall without Beams

进入东二道门，中心大殿即斋宫的正殿，因是完全采用砖瓦砌成而得名"无梁殿"。无梁殿五间，庑殿顶绿琉璃筒瓦，明间是皇帝斋戒期间召见大臣的地方，中设皇帝宝座，后护木质屏风，上精雕四季山水，宝座上悬匾书"钦若昊天"。次间和稍间分别是大臣休息和等待陪祀时刻到来的场所。

大殿丹墀左边是铜人亭，铜人亭石质，高逾丈，亭内有石座，每逢皇帝斋戒时，执事人员将手执斋戒牌的铜人（高约57厘米）置于亭内，目的是提醒皇帝恪守戒律。

丹墀右边是时辰亭，祭天祈谷的时间是日出前七刻，相当于凌晨4点15分，届时由太常寺堂官和钦天监官员将时辰奏折送入亭内，再由首领太监取出，呈报皇帝，皇帝起驾临坛行礼。

铜人亭
The Pavilion of Fasting Bronze Figurine

There is also an imperial throne inside it. Above the throne hang antithetical couplets, which read "Listen attentively and clearly to ancestors' teachings before doing practice and drawing up plans, and do not detest farming before knowing the hardships of sowing and reaping", and the horizontal scroll bears the inscription of "Zhuang Jing Ri Qiang" The antithetical couplets fully reflect the two virtues of valuing agriculture and respecting ancestors in the ancient time in our country. This hall facing east is also the main hall. In the south is the fast bedroom for praying for rain in summer, and in the north is the warm room for worshipping Heaven in winter. The warm room is furnished with golden stoves and heated brick bed. And on writing desks lie four treasures of the study and thread bound Chinese books. The environment of the rooms is solemn and comfortable; the arrangement of them is simple and elegant while is still of imperial honor and splendor.

Except the halls for the emperor to work, live and sleep, in the Fasting Palace there are also the Head Eunuch's (*Zhishoufang*), House (*Jiuyifang*), Custodian House (*Dianshoufang*), Imperial Kitchen (*Yushanfang*), and Cha Guo Fang (houses for preparing tea and fruit), Yi Bao Fang (houses that are used for storing paper bags, paper garments and paper money as offerings to the dead), and so on. It is a "mini palace" not only in name but in reality as well.

During the fast, the emperor in the Fasting Palace in the Temple of Heaven took no

寝宫明间内景
An Inner Sight of the Room the Door of Which
Opens Directly onto the Courtyard in the Bedroom

寝宫明间内景
An Inner Sight of the Room the Door of Which
Opens Directly onto the Courtyard in the Bedroom

　　正殿后面是皇帝斋戒时的寝宫,亦有皇帝宝座,上悬联:"克践厥猷聪听祖考之彝训,无敦康事先知稼穑之艰难",横批"庄敬日强"。这副对联充分体现了我国古代祭天重农、尊祖的两大特点。寝宫和正殿一样,坐西朝东,南为夏季祈雨时的斋戒卧室,北为冬季祭天时的暖房,备有金炉暖炕,书案上陈文房四宝,线装书籍,室内气氛肃穆却不乏舒适,布置淡雅仍不失帝王富贵。

　　除了皇帝办公、居住的正殿、寝殿,斋宫内还有首领太监值守房、纠仪房、典守房、御膳房、茶果房、衣包房等建筑,是名副其实的"小皇宫"。

notice of laws and prosecutions, didn't work (except in very urgent situations), listened to music, went into the inner bedroom, visited patients, condoled, drank, ate fistular onions, Chinese chives, scallions, or garlic, prayed, offered sacrifices to God, or swept the grave (pay respect at a person's tomb). The emperor needed to bath on the day before the Heaven worship ceremony. There used to be a bathroom to the south of the Sleeping Hall. However, today even its ruin cannot be found.

The main hall, Sleeping Hall, Watch House and Belfry in the Fasting Palace have been restored to its original appearance during the reign of Emperor Qianlong in Qing dynasty. The lifelike wax statue of Emperor Qianlong is displayed in the main hall, and poems delineating the scene of Heaven worship written by Emperor Qianlong also hang on the wall.

皇帝斋戒居住的卧室
The Bedroom Where the Emperors
Live during the Fastbefore Praying for Rain

无梁殿内景
An Inner Sight of the Hall without Beams

　　皇帝在天坛斋宫斋戒期间，"不理刑名，不办事(有要紧事依旧办理)，不听音乐，不入内寝，不问疾，不吊丧，不饮酒，不食葱韭薤蒜，不祈祷，不祭神，不扫墓"。斋戒前一日沐浴，斋宫寝殿南侧旧时建有浴室，今已无遗址可寻。

　　斋宫内正殿、寝殿、值守房、钟楼等处古迹，现已按照清乾隆时期原貌恢复。

三、神秘的祭台——圜丘台

Mysterious Sacrificing Altar: Circular Mound Altar

圜丘台远景
A Far Sight of the Circular Mound

　　出斋宫东门一直向东来到南北向大道上，向南望去，一座三门并立组成的大门在不远处屹立，这门俗称"三座门"，穿过这道门，就来到了圜丘坛。

1. 圜丘坛

　　圜丘坛始建于明嘉靖九年（1530 年），当年建造的圜丘台较今天的略小而高一些，台面以青色琉璃砖铺墁，周围栏板柱子皆青色琉璃。清乾隆十四年（1749年），加以扩建。工程历时三年多，改建后的圜丘台比明代的更加宽阔壮观，台面改用艾叶青石，栏板使用汉白玉，一直保留至今。

　　圜丘坛有四门，东西南北分别为泰元门、昭亨门、广利门、成贞门，四门取义《易经》的"乾"卦卦辞，"乾，元亨利贞"。成贞门位于圜丘坛与祈谷坛的分界墙

I f you walk out from the East Gate of the Fasting Palace, go eastward until you get to a main road connecting north and south, and see southward, you will see a huge gate consisting of three gates in a distance. This huge gate is generally called "Triple Gate".Going through this gate, you will get to the Circular Mound Altar.

1. Circular Mound Altar

The Circular Mound Altar was originally built in the ninth year during the reign of Emperor Jiajing in Ming dynasty (in 1530). At that time the Circular Mound Altar was a little smaller and higher than the one we see today, and its surface was paved with grey glazed bricks. The balustrades and pillars were also covered with grey glazed tiles. In the 14th year during the reign of Emperor Qianlong in Qing dynasty (in 1749), it was extended. After three years of reconstruction, the new Circular Mound Altar became grander and more magnificent. The surface of the altar was paved with Artemisia leaf grey marbles, while the balustrades were made of white marble. This appearance has been maintained till now.

The Circular Mound Altar has four gates, which are Taiyuan Gate in the east, Zhaoheng Gate in the west, Guangli Gate in the south, and Chengzhen Gate in the north. The four gates get their names from the explanation of the meaning of the Qian Diagram (the first of the Eight Diagrams) in *Yi Jing* (*Book of Changes*), which said "*Qian means Yuan* (Heaven), *Heng* (Prosperity), *Li* (Interest), and *Zhen* (Honesty)", The Chengzhen Gate is in the middle of the circular part of the wall, which divides the Circular Mound Altar and the Altar of Prayer for Good Harvests. The Chengzhen Gate is straight in the east and west parts but circular in the middle. This kind of shape implies the ancient peopl's belief that "The sky is circular and the earth is square" and it is in accordance with the design that the walls of the Temple of Heaven and the Temple of Earth are circular in the north and square in the south. If you go out from the altar through the Chengzhen Gate, you will be on the sacred way leading to the Hall of Prayer for Good Harvestss. The Triple Gate and the Chengzhen Gate are in the same wall, which is for the convenience of the Emperor to enter or leave the Fasting Palace.

In those years the Emperor would get out of his Imperial Sedan at the Zhaoheng Gate and take Liyu (a smaller carriage for ceremony carried by 12 people) instead before he went to the altar to hold the Heaven worship rites. Thousands of people

上,这段分界墙东西段保持平直,只在中心段向北凸起成弧形,成贞门即在这段弧形墙正中,"天圆地方"的含义寓意其中,也与天地墙北圆南方相一致。北出成贞门即踏上通往祈年殿的神道。三座门与成贞门在一道墙上,是为方便皇帝出入斋宫而建的。

　　当年皇帝祭天时先到昭亨门降辇,由玉辇换乘12人抬的小轿——礼舆。几千人的队伍在昭亨门外停下等待皇帝完成这一礼仪。我们从斋宫过三座门前行到圜丘坛南坛墙(也是天坛内坛墙)东行,即来到昭亨门。

2. 圜丘台

　　从昭亨门北望,圜丘台即在眼前。圜丘台又称祭天台、拜天台,是圜丘坛的主体建筑,是天坛最成功的建筑之一,最撼人心魄的是它的神秘,臆想中人类与天神朦胧接触所应具备的一切氛围,圜丘台都具备了。它的建造完全照应古人

建在圜丘坛内墙圆墙上的棂星门
The Star-Worshipping Gate Built in the Inner Circular Wall of the Circular Mound

would stop outside the Zhaoheng Gate and wait until the emperor finished the rites. Starting from the Fasting Palace, walking through the Triple Gate towards the southern wall of the altar, and then going eastward, you will get to the Zhaoheng Gate.

2. Circular Mound Altar Platform

Looking northward from the South Gate, you will see the Circular Mound Platform, which is also called Heaven Sacrifice Platform, or Heaven Worship Platform. It is the main building of the Circular Mound Altar and the most successful building in the Temple of Heaven. It is so mysterious that people can have a vague imagination that they can communicate with gods. Its construction is absolutely in accordance with the ancient people's belief of "circular heaven and square earth" Heaven belongs to yang while Earth belongs to yin. The Circular Mound Altar is located at the most yang place of yang places, which is at the Xun diagram of Eight Diagrams in the southeast of the capital, and numbers concerning this altar are all yang, namely 9 or multiples of 9. This altar shows its builders' simple but vivid view of the world. Through this building the builders also expressed their great respect to gods and their strong desire to get integrated with heaven. It is a masterpiece of buildings and landscape designs.

"天圆地方"之说。天为阳,地为阴,圜丘坛的选址也按古人"阳中之阳"的观念,选在都城的东南方巽位,各种数据也极尽之阳数,即9或9的倍数。建造者通过圜丘坛反映了当时朴素而鲜明的世界观,表达了对天神的无限尊崇和渴望达到天人合一境界的强烈愿望,是建筑和景观设计的杰作。

圜丘坛有两道墙墙环绕,外方形,内圆形,两重墙皆红墙蓝瓦,内外四面都设棂星门,共24座,石造,上饰云版,下嵌抱鼓,造型优美,富有韵律,有"云门玉立"之称。

内、外棂星门相对
The Inner and Outer Star-Worshipping Gate Stand Facing Each Other

The Circular Mound Altar is enclosed within two walls, a square wall outside a round one. They are both red walls covered with blue tiles. Each contains four groups of Star – worshipping Gate with 24 marble doors altogether, which are decorated with Yunban (a kind of percussion instrument, made of long strips of iron sheet and used in the old times to give the correct time or announce an event) and Baogu (another kind of percussion instrument). The shape is exquisite and of rich rhythms, and thus gets the name of "Erecting Clouds Gates" (*Yunmenyuli*).

3. Heavenly Center Stone

The Circular Mound Altar has three terraces, and each of them has four entrances and a flight leading down in every direction. The surface of the altar is paved by Artemisia leaf gray marbles. Its size, shape and style have profound implications. In the center of the upper terrace there is a raised round marble, which is called "Heavenly Center Stone" or "Supreme Ultimate Stone". If people stand on this stone and speak, there will be a strong effect of acoustic resonance, as if people are communicating with gods. This is mysteriously wonderful. This phenomenon has existed since it was built during Emperor Jiajing's reign in Ming dynasty. At that time when the official read aloud prayers to the God of Heaven, his voice was loud and resonant as if he was communicating with gods. People were thought to be able to get integrated with Heaven at that moment. Therefore this stone was named the "Yi Zhao Jing Cong" Stone.

"In the center of the Circular Mound Altar where the Heavenly Center Stone is located is the central point of the Circular Mound Altar. When people stand on this stone, the voices can spread to every direction. Below the Circular Mound Altar

圜丘台面上的天心石及
以9为倍数的艾叶青石
*The Heavenly Center Stone
on the Circular Mound and
the Artemisia Leaf
Gray Marbles the Number
of Which Is Multiple of 9*

天心石保护石
The Stones Protecting the Heavenly Center Stone

3. 天心石

圜丘台有三层，各层四面出陛，台面俱铺墁艾叶青石，圜丘台的规制寓意颇深，上层台面中心有一圆石，称之"天心石"，又称"太极石"，人站在天心石上讲话，有很强的共鸣效果，玄妙万端，似人与自然在对话。明嘉靖朝建圜丘台时，这种现象就已存在，当时读祝官在此诵读给皇天上帝的祝辞，声音翁鸣，仿佛与天神交流，天人合一的境界由此达到。这块圆石遂被命名为"亿兆景从"石。

"圜丘台中心圆石'天心石'的位置，是圜丘台的中心点，人站在上面讲话，声音通过空气向四面八方传播，圜丘台下面有高度不同的护栏及形状不同的围墙，

Platform there are guardrails with various height and walls of different shapes. The sound waves spread out and meet obstructions at different distances, so the time the sound waves need to return varies, and there are many echoes. Therefore it seems that there are more than one people speaking. If people don't stand on this stone while speaking, the sound waves spread out, scatter disorderly and don't assemble, and then there will be no echo." This is an early explanation for the echo phenomenon of the Heavenly Center Stone.

Nine concentric rings of fan–shaped stones surround the Heavenly Center Stone. The number of stones in the first ring is 9, in the second 18, and so on, up to 81 in the 9th ring. The middle and bottom terraces also have 9 rings each. Even the numbers of the carved balustrades on these terraces are also the multiples of 9. Nine was the largest heavenly number accessible to man. Some people think this design implies the nine layers of heaven. Today it has existed more than 460 years since the Circular Mound Altar was built. A scholar from Taiwan uses the five colors of write, blue, black, red and yellow to symbolize metal, wood, water, fire and earth, and he explains that taiji (Supreme Ultimate) is the Heavenly Center Stone. Therefore, he draws a conclusion that the structure of the Circular Mound Altar consists with Chinese ancient He Luo Xiang Shu and the rhythms of bagua (Eight Diagrams), which vividly expresses our ancestors' traditional concept.

4. Historic Sites Insider the Outer Wall of Circular Mound Altar Such as Firewood Stove(Fanchailu),Yi Kan and Burning Stove etc.

Firewood Stoveis for incinerating the sacrifices offered to the God of Heaven at the firewood–burning rite. It is built with green glazed round bricks. On the east, west and south sides, there are 9 steps leading to the burner. On the north side, it is the mouth of the burner, through which firewood can be sent into the burner's chamber. Only during the Heaven worship rite did people hold this firewood burning rite. Therefore, the Firewood Stove in the Temple of Heaven is unique. The

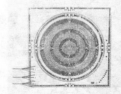

圜丘坛图
A View of the Circular Mound

声波传递出去遇到远近不同的障碍返回的时间不同,因此不是一个回声。站在中心圆石上讲话,发出的声音遇到四面圆形护栏时,同时返回形成好像不止一个人说话的现象。如果不站在中心圆石上讲话,则声音发出后涣散不集中,没有回声。"这是对圜丘台天心石回音产生原因的较早解释。

围绕"天心石"的以扇面形状铺开的石板均以9的倍数递增,第一重为9块,第二重为18块,直到第九重为81块。下面两层台面的石板和四周的栏板也都是以9的倍数递增。每层的台阶也是9级,9是至阳数,也有说这意味着"九重天"。在圜丘台建成之后460多年的今天,台湾的一位学者用白、蓝、黑、红、黄五种颜色代表金、木、水、火、土,太极即是天心石,表明圜丘台的建造与中国古代的河洛象数及八卦韵律相一致,是我们祖先传统观念的形象表述。

4. 圜丘坛外壝墙内有燔柴炉、瘗坎、燎炉等古迹

燔柴炉是为举行燔柴礼时焚烧献给皇天上帝供品而设。燔柴炉,圆形,绿琉璃砖砌造,东西南三面均砌台阶各9级,以备向炉内投放供品。北面则为炉膛开口,以备添柴。燔柴礼为祭天所独有,因而燔柴炉亦为天坛独具,古人认为天神居于太空,人们祭祀神灵供献的玉帛牺牲在燔柴炉内化作烟气升至太空,神便是享受到了人间的礼献。祭天仪式第一项即为"燔柴迎帝神",焚烧时炉上有燎牛,香气冲天,皇帝位于燔柴炉西的望燎位行望燎礼,心中默祷祈愿实现。

燔柴炉
Firewood Stove

ancient people thought that gods were living in heaven, so people offered jade objects, silk fabrics and sacrifices to Heaven by putting them in the Firewood Stoveand incinerating them. The sacrifices were incinerated in the burner, turned into smoke and gas, and went up into the sky. It was thought that it meant that gods in Heaven received the human world's sacrifices. The first thing in the agenda of Heaven worship is to "burn fire wood to welcome gods" A sacrificial calf was being barbecued in the burner and the scent pervaded all around to the sky. At that time, the Emperor stood at the Burn Watching Place on the west side of the burner to perform the burn watching rite and pray in silence.

Yi Kan is a pit where animal sacrifice's hair and blood are buried. It is on the east side of the Firewood Stove. It is also built with green glazed bricks. It is round in shape and its diameter is less than 1 meter and its depth is about 30 centimeters. Burning Stove(also a kind of burner) is openwork made of pig iron with six feet. It is used exclusively for incinerating tribute at the memorial tablets on the flanks. There are eight *Peiwei* (accompany position, enshrining memorial tablets of ancestors) for the eight emperors from Emperor Nurhachi to Emperor Daoguang, which are set up during Emperor Xianfeng's reign in Qing dynasty, and four

燎炉 Burning Stove

瘞坎
Yikan

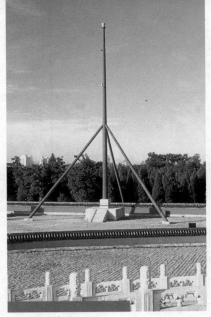

复建的望灯杆
The Posts of Watching Lights
Which Have Been Rebuilt

瘞坎在燔柴炉以东,是瘞埋牺牲毛血的所在,也是由绿琉璃砌造而成,圆形,直径不足1米,深约0.3米。

燎炉,镂空六足,生铁铸造,专门用来焚烧祭天时配位、从位前供奉的供品。圜丘坛有8个配位,是清咸丰朝规制(即清咸丰朝供奉的自努尔哈赤到道光的前8代皇帝),从位8个(即日月星辰、风云雷雨、周天星宿、金木水火土,因而铁燎炉共计12座)。燎炉由清太祖努尔哈赤神位向下依次向东排列,从位燎炉则分别放置在圜丘坛东西棂星门内西侧。当年行祭礼时,燔柴炉要烧掉两千多斤木柴,每个铁燎炉也要烧掉近一千斤木柴。

圜丘坛外墙墙内西南隅有望灯,最初望灯仅一个,明崇祯年间增至3座。直至民国三年(1914年),袁世凯祭天时拆掉两根灯杆,留下中间一根,现存望灯台遗迹两座。灯杆高9丈9尺,据说天高9重9丈9尺。灯杆上悬巨大灯笼,高逾2米。在寒冷的冬夜,一盏高悬的望灯,燔柴炉冲天的浓烟,灯影云烟,伴随钟磬空灵,充满了对天帝的虔诚,对祖宗的尊崇。

Congwei (following position, enshrining another kind of memorial tablets) dedicated to the gods of Sun, Moon, and Stars; the gods of Wind, Cloud, Thunder, and Rain; the gods of Constellations in the sky; and the gods of five elements (metal, wood, water, fire and earth). Therefore, there are altogether 12 Burning Stoves. These Burning Stoves lined up eastward from Emperor Nurhachi's memorial tablet. The four burners at Congwei are placed at the west side inside the east and west Star – worshipping Gates. When the emperor performed the heaven worship rite, over 2000 *jin* (1000 Kg) wood would be burned up in the Fire Wood Burner, and near1000 *jin* (500 Kg) wood would be burned up in each Burning Stove.

Watching Lights (*Wangdeng*) is located at the southwest corner of the outer wall of the Circular Mound Altar. At first there was only one lantern. During the reign of Emperor Chongzhen in Ming dynasty, two more lanterns were added. However, during the period of Republic of China, Yuan Shikai pulled down two Bases of Watching Lights when he worshiped Heaven. Now only the lantern in the middle and the vestiges of two lantern stands are left. The lantern post is 9 *zhang* and 9

祭祀的时刻是在日出前七刻（凌晨4点15分），冬至的这天此刻是黎明前的黑暗，天色漆黑，为了照明和渲染气氛，除瞭望灯，祭坛上下灯具很多，设于道途两侧，用以照路，数千盏灯具把祭坛装扮得神奇而幽幻。这些灯具种类不一，名称各异，神位前左右陈设金丝羊角灯、红纸插灯，将坛上的陈设照得通明，便于皇帝及执事行礼。照亮祭坛中心通往四周道路的用灯，就是所谓"坛上灯"，其中朝灯似小屋大小，高1.5米左右，内燃红蜡烛，还有各色红、黄、蓝纸插灯。用在殿内台阶两侧及台阶下的小灯，大不盈尺，俗名"庙儿灯"。史书形容当时祭坛上下及周围数千盏灯具的壮观景象时称"一灯亮，万灯明，灿如列星"，可以想见祭天大典时，周围漆黑一片，而坛上是烛光摇曳，望灯高悬，充满了神秘色彩，更增添了祭祀气氛。

　　乾隆四十七年（1782年），因京师、保定一带数月无雨，禾苗枯槁，在天坛举行了常雩礼。皇帝行礼时只见坛内悬挂的天灯仅二盏，少挂了一盏，传谕查办有关人员"查明革职，发往伊犁效力赎罪"，对负责验收祭天准备工作的官员也下令一一议处。神位除了灯具不可或缺，圜丘坛上最重要的陈设恐怕就是神位了。

禋祀图

燔柴升煙歆若昊
天乃大報本
返始也

禋祀图 The Picture of Heaven Worshipping in Qing Dynasty

chi (33 meters) high, because it was believed that heaven had 9 layers with a height of 9 *zhang* and 9 *chi*. A huge lantern hung over 2 meters high at the post. At the heaven worship ceremony at a cold winter night, after the high Watching Lights were lit, with dense smoke coming out from the Firewood Stove and rising up into the sky, and with indescribably free sound from the Belfry and musicians, people prayed with devout reverence to Heaven and ancestors.

The time to offer sacrifices and pray for good harvests is seven quarters before the sunrise, (a quarter past four before dawn). At this time in winter, it is quite dark. For illumination and to play up the environment, there are many other lanterns except the Watching Lights. Decked out in thousands of lanterns, the sacrificing altar looked mysterious and profound. These lanterns are of various kinds and had different names. In front of gods' memorial tablets are Jinsi Yangjiao Lanterns (a kind of lantern decorated by gold thread and in a shape of a ram's horn) and red paper lanterns, which illuminate the displays on the altar quite well, so as to make it more convenient for the emperor and officials on duty to perform rites. Yong Lantern is used to illuminate the paths around the altar and it is also called "Lantern on Altar". Chao Lantern is as big as a cabin, which is about 1.5 meters high with red candles lit in it. There were also many paper lanterns with different colors such as red, yellow, blue, etc. Below the steps of the Circular Mound Altar and on the sacred path there are many small lanterns with diameters less than 1 *chi* (1 *chi*=1/3 meter), which are generally called "Miao'er Lantern". According to historical records, when thousands of lanterns around the altar were lit, the scene was so grand that the records described it as follows: "one lantern shines and ten thousand lanterns light like stars in the sky". We can imagine how grand and mysterious the scene was and how solemn the rite was when the altar was bright with flickering candles' light and high-hung Watching Lights while all around was dark at night.

In the 47th year during Emperor Qianlong's reign, because it had not rained for several months in the capital and Baoding, the emperor held a ceremony praying for rain. When he was performing the rites, he saw there were only two Heaven Lanterns hanging in the altar while there should be three lanterns. He relayed the imperial instruction that the officials who were in charge of the three lanterns should be prosecuted and "be dismissed and exiled to farm to atone for their crime" and the officials who were on duty to check the preparation for Heaven worship should

皇穹宇
The Imperial Vault of Heaven

"皇天上帝"设在圜丘坛第一层正中的位置,所用的幄帐是一座圆形大帐篷,南向。东西两翼陈放配位神位,所用的幄帐是长方形的,东西各一座,内设清太祖努尔哈赤以下的8位祖先神位(咸丰朝),按左昭右穆为序排列,东西相向。圜丘坛第二层设从位,即大明、夜明、星辰、风云雷雨的从祀神位,是四座天青色方形幄帐。大明、夜明神各居一幄,星辰、风云雷雨各居一幄。每一神位前都摆着登、笾、豆、簋、爵、尊、俎等祭器,内盛以各种祭品。

5. 皇穹宇

站在圜丘台北望,皇穹宇尽收眼底,皇穹宇有三座拱券式琉璃宫门,门上彩画黄绿相间,精美别致,是北京城仅有的几处琉璃彩画之一。

51

瓷铏, 祭天礼器,
陈设于从祀位,
内盛和羹
*Xin, the Sacrificial
Vessel Displayed
in the Following
Position with
Hegeng in It*

瓷豆, 祭天礼器,
陈设于正、配位,
内盛肉醢
*Dou, the Sacrificial
Vessel Displayed
in the Main and
Accompanying
Position with
Rouhai in It*

瓷簋, 祭天礼器,
陈设于正、配位,
内盛黍、稷
*Fu, the Sacrificial
Vessel Displayed
in the Main and
Accompanying
Position with
Shu and Ji in It*

also be punished.Memorial tablets (*Shenwei*) are the most important displays on the altar except lanterns.

"God of Heaven" is located at the central place surrounded by a huge round tent facing south on the first floor of the Circular Mound Altar. On the east side and west side the memorial tablets of Peiwei are displayed and enclosed with a square tent on each side. These memorial tablets are for the eight ancestors from Emperor Nurhachi to Emperor Daoguang, lined up according to an order in ancient patriarchal clan system (the first ancestor's memorial tablet lies in center, the second, fourth, sixth and so on lie in left, and the third, fifth, seventh and so on lie in right). The tablets in the east and west face each other. On the second floor of the Circular Mound Altar are displayed memorial tablets of Congwei, namely the tablets of gods of *Daming* (Sun), *Yeming* (Moon), Stars, Wind, Cloud, Thunder, and Rain, and they are surrounded by four azure square tents. One tent is for the god of Daming, one for the god of Yeming, one for god of stars, and one for gods of wind, cloud, thunder and rain. In front of each tablet are displayed the sacrificial utensils such as *Deng* (a sacrificial vessel), *Xing* (a sacrificial utensil), *Bian* (a bamboo utensil), *Dou* (a standing cup), *Gui* (a round– mouthed food vessel with two or four loop handles), *Fu* (a square bamboo receptacle), *Jue* (an ancient wine vessel with three legs and a loop handle), *Zun* (a kind of wine vessel), *Zu* (a sacrificial utensil), with sacrifices in them.

5. Imperial Vault of Heaven

Looking northward from the Circular Mound Altar, the whole scene of the Imperial Vault of Heaven comes into view. The Imperial Vault of Heaven has three arched glazed gates with exquisite paintings in alternating yellow and green colors. This is one of the few buildings, which have glazed colorful paintings in Beijing.

皇穹宇院落
The Courtyard of the Imperial Vault of Heaven

　　皇穹宇原名泰神殿,建成后不久就改名为皇穹宇。皇穹宇是存放祭天神牌的场所,蓝琉璃瓦单檐攒尖顶,东西南三面出阶,前开三门,殿前丹陛石刻有二龙戏珠图案,台基周围汉白玉栏板。大殿由8根檐柱环绕支撑,3层镏金斗拱,层层上叠,天花层层收缩,藻井内有团龙一条,金光闪烁,金柱沥粉贴金缠枝莲,大殿内外施龙凤和玺彩画,富丽堂皇。

　　大殿正中陈设"皇天上帝"神版,青饰金书,满汉合璧,被供奉在金龙神龛内。龛前9级木阶梯,后护金龙屏风,下面石须弥座前有9级石阶,供案上设五供。大殿两侧设皇帝列祖列宗配位神牌,现大殿内按咸丰朝规制恢复历史原貌,陈设有配位8座。

Originally, the Imperial Vault of Heaven was named as The Hall for Appeasing Gods (*Taishendian*). After being finished, it was renamed as Imperial Vault of Heaven. It is where memorial tablets are kept. It is covered by blue glazed tiles characterized by a cone-shaped roof with single eave. It has staircase on the east side, west side and south side, and three doors in the front. The Danbi Marble (a gigantic carved marble ramp laid in the stone staircase leading up to the front entrance) in front of the hall is carved in "Two Dragons Playing with a Pearl" design. The base of the hall is surrounded by white marble balustrades. The main hall is buttressed by 8 eave columns in a circle. On top of the columns there are three layers of gilt brackets supporting a circular caisson, or covered ceiling. Each higher layer is smaller than the lower one. The caisson ceiling is characterized by a golden coiling dragon design, which is glittering and glistening. The 8 pillars are painted scarlet and decorated with golden lotuses. Inside and outside the main hall, there are colorful paintings of dragon, phoenix and royal seal, with which the hall is decorated sumptuously.

In the middle of the main hall the memorial tablet of "God of Heaven" is displayed, on which gold words are written. It is a combination of the Man nationality's culture and the Han's culture. It is enshrined in the golden dragon shrine. In front of the shrine there is a 9-step wood flight, and behind it there is a golden dragon-folding screen. Below the shrine there is a marble Buddha's Statue. In front of the marble Buddha's Statue there is a 9-step stone flight. On the altar table five oblation utensils are offered. On both

皇穹宇内景 The Inner Sight of the Imperial Vault of Heaven

55

从祀位供奉的神牌
The Memorial Tablets Enshrined in the Following Position

配位供奉的康熙神版
The Memorial Tablet of Kangxi Enshrined in the Accompanying Position

sides of the hall, memorial tablets of royal ancestors are displayed. Today the hall has been restored to its original appearance during the reign of Emperor Xianfeng in Qing dynasty. There are eight memorial tablets of Peiwei displayed in it.

In front of the Imperial Vault of Heaven, there are one side hall on the east side and one on the right side. The memorial tablets of Congwei are kept in them. In the east side hall, memorial tablets of "God of *Daming* (God of Sun), God of Big Dipper, God of Wood, Fire, Earth, Metal and Water, God of 28 constellations, God of Stars" are displayed; and in the west side hall, "God of *Yeming* (God of Moon), God of Cloud, God of Rain, God of Wind, God of Thunder" are displayed. At the fifth watch just before dawn on the day of offering sacrifices, all these memorial tablets and the tablets of "God of Heaven" and royal ancestors in the main hall of the Imperial Vault of Heaven are enshrined in the Dragon Pavilion and carried to the Circular Mound Altar in a order that the memorial tablet of God of Heaven is at the forefront, then the tablets of Peiwei, and finally the tablets of Congwei, waiting the emperor's arrival and performance of the sacrificial ceremony.

The most important thing in a sacrificial ceremony is the arrangement of memorial tablets. In every dynasty there were strict rules. The memorial tablets are divided into three classes, namely *Zhengwei* (main position), Peiwei, and *Congwei*. Today the main hall and side halls of the Imperial Vault of Heaven have been restored to its original appearance according to the rules established during the reign of

皇穹宇东配殿内景
The Inner Sight of the East Annex Hall in the Imperial Vault of Heaven

　　皇穹宇殿前东西各有配庑一座,是存放圜丘台祭天从祀牌位的地方。东配庑供奉"大明之神(太阳神)、北斗七星之神、木火土金水之神、二十八宿之神、周天星辰之神";西配庑供奉"夜明之神(月神)、云师之神、雨师之神、风伯之神、雷师之神"。大祀当日五鼓时分,这些从祀神位同皇穹宇正殿的皇天上帝、列祖列宗神位一同分别奉于龙亭之内,按上帝在前,配位、从位依次在后的顺序,抬至圜丘台,等待皇帝驾到举行大典。

　　祭礼中最重要的是祭天神位的设置,对此各朝都有极严格的定制,神位分三等:即正位、配位、从位。现皇穹宇正殿、配庑按清咸丰朝规制恢复了历史原貌,游人可看到不同质地、不同颜色的神版和神牌,神亦有等。

Emperor Xianfeng in Qing dynasty. Visitors can see different memorial tablets of different quality and different color, which indicate that even gods are hierarchical.

There are four major acoustic buildings in China. Compared with the other three buildings, the Temple of Heaven was built latest and because of its acoustic effects, it ranks first among the four.

The wall surrounding the Imperial Vault of Heaven is the world–famous Echo Wall. The Echo Wall is made of the bricks in Linqing city in Shandong. The bricks are laid seam to seam. The Linqing bricks are fine and of close texture. If you knock at it, you can hear a sound, and if you break it, there won't be any holes. The Echo Wall is also called "Sound Spreading Wall" .If people face north and speak toward the wall, the sound wave will echo along the round smooth wall and be spread to a place far away. Even when two people stand respectively behind the east side hall and the west side hall and there are two halls and a distance of over 60 meters between them, they can still hear each other's voice as clearly as using a telephone.

The Triple Sounds Stone (*Sanxinshi*) in the Imperial Vault of Heaven also has

皇穹宇院落的围墙即举世闻名的回音壁
The Enclosing Wall of the Courtyard of the Imperial Vault of Heaven Is the Renowned Echo Wall

　　我国有四大声学建筑，与其他三处相比，天坛具有声学效应的建筑最终建成年代最晚，但天坛以声学现象众多，声学效果明显而位居四大声学建筑首位。

　　皇穹宇的围墙就是举世闻名的**回音壁**，回音壁使用的是山东临清城砖磨砖

具有回音的"三音石"
The Triple Sounds Stone with
Resounding Effect

marvelous echo effects. If you stand on the first flagstone on the sacred path outside of the main hall's door of the Imperial Vault of Heaven and clap once, you will hear one echo. If you stand on the second flagstone, you will hear two echoes. If you stand on the third flagstone, you will hear three echoes. And if you stand on the fourth and fifth flagstone, you can also hear echoes. The Triple Sounds Stone was once named as a historical vestige of "Earth Whisper, Heaven Thunder". It was believed that Heaven's sharp eyes could perceive every word and every behavior in human world clearly.

The Dialogue Stone (*Duihuashi*) is found in a research test in 1995. If you stand on the third flagstone from south to north on the paved path leading to the main hall in the Imperial Vault of Heaven, you will clearly hear the voice of the people at the northeast corner of east side hall (or the northwest corner of the west side hall). If two people stand respectively at the two positions, they can communicate clearly with each other in normal sound volume, even the environment around them is quite noisy. This finding caused a sensation. Our ancestor's talent is surprising and miraculous. The Temple of Heaven deserves to be called a huge treasure house

对缝砌成,临清砖质地细密,敲之有声,断之无孔。回音壁又称"传声墙",人面向北对墙说话,声波沿着光滑的圆形围墙连续反射,可以传到很远的地方。两人分别站在东西配庑后,距离60多米,中间还有两座大殿相隔,说话声音却如同打电话一样清晰。

三音石 皇穹宇的三音石回音现象很奇妙,人站在皇穹宇正殿门外神道第一块石板上击掌可以听到一声回音,站在第二块石板上击掌,可以听到两声回音,第三块石板则可听到三声回音,站在第四、第五块石板上击掌,也能听到回音。皇穹宇的"三音石"曾被命名为"人间私语,天闻若雷"的古迹,仿佛人间人们的一言一行,冥冥之中自有天神明察秋毫。

对话石 1995年在研究测试过程中,又发现了一处新的"对话石"声学现象。人站在皇穹宇内中心甬道上从南数第三块石板上,可以清晰地听到东配庑东北角(或西配庑西北角)的声音,两人分别站在上述位置,用普通音量可以清楚地交谈,即便是在十分嘈杂的情况下,仍然很清晰。这一发现引起了轰动,古人的聪明才智令人惊讶不已。天坛不愧是一座巨大的宝库,有许多奥秘待人们去发现和揭开。

奇妙的"对话石"
The Wonderful Dialogue Stone

61

and it still has profound mysteries waiting to be explored.

6. Subsidiary Buildings in the Circular Mound Altar

Looking eastward from the Circular Mound Altar, you will see some other buildings hidden among the trees and green tiles and red walls. They are far from main buildings and stand still in the depth of cypress trees. It is these buildings that set off the conspicuousness and sublimity of the Circular Mound Altar. These are the subsidiary buildings of the Circular Mound Altar, including Divine Kitchen (*Shenchu*), Divine Storehouse (*Shengku*), Triple Houses (*Sanku*), and Butcher House (*Zaishengting*).

Divine Kitchen and **Divine Storehouse** are in the same courtyard. The Divine Storehouse facing south is used to store the already finished tributes. The Divine Kitchen is a place where tributes are prepared. Each of them has five rooms. They are covered by green glazed round tiles and located at the mountaintop. In the courtyard there is a well house, whose roof is of a hexagon shape and covered by green glazed tiles. This is used to provide water for tributes.

Triple Houses are in another courtyard at the east side of the courtyard of Divine Kitchen and Divine Storehouse. In this courtyard, there are Musical Instruments House (*Yueqiku*), Zongjian House (*Zongjianku*), and Sacrificial Utensil House (*Jiqiku*) from north to south. Each House has three rooms and faces west. They are all also covered by green glazed round tiles and located at the mountaintop. At ordinary times musical instruments, sacrificial utensils and zongjian (brown straw mat) were kept respectively in the Triple Houses, and only when a sacrificial ceremony was performed would they be taken out.

Butcher House is located at the east side of the Divine Kitchen. At the southeast corner inside its courtyard door there is a well house. Its main hall is located at the mountaintop with double eaves and covered by green round glazed tiles. It has three rooms. The main room has a door, the secondary room has sill wall and grilles, and there are lattice windows in the gable walls on the east and west side. Two stages stand both in front of and behind the hall. And there is a kitchen behind the back eave wall.

Ancient cypress trees: Having visited all the ancient buildings in the Circular Mound Altar, let's have a look at the ancient trees around. Some cypress trees are

南宰牲亭
South Butcher House

6. 圜丘坛附属建筑

站在圜丘台东望,有绿瓦红墙隐蔽在树丛中,它们远离主体建筑,静静伫立在柏林深处,越发烘托出圜丘坛醒目崇高的地位。这组建筑就是圜丘坛的附属建筑——神厨、神库、三库、宰牲亭。

神厨、神库共一院落,神库坐北朝南,用于贮放制作完成的供品,神厨坐东朝西,专用于制作供品,两座大殿均为五开间绿琉璃筒瓦歇山顶。院内有井亭,绿琉璃瓦六角顶,做供品汲水之用。

神厨、神库院东即**三库院**,院内由北向南依次为乐器库、棕荐库、祭器库,每库三间,坐东朝西,绿琉璃筒瓦硬山顶。平时祭祀用乐器、祭器、棕荐即分别收贮在三库,祭礼时取出使用。

宰牲亭院落在神厨院东,门内东南隅有井亭。大殿重檐歇山顶,绿琉璃筒瓦,三开间,明间设门,次间槛墙为格窗,东西两山墙皆碎格棱窗,前后有台,后檐墙有灶火间。

so strange in their shapes that they arouse people's rich associations. A cypress called "**Wentian Cypress**" on the southwest side of the Echo Wall has a branch on its top pointing straight up toward the sky, as if it was Quyuan with high hat and wide waist belt interrogating the Heaven full of grief and indignation, asking, "Heaven, you enjoy the boundless reverence from the human world, but have you removed any unfairness from the human world" This cypress lives outside the wall of the Imperial Vault of Heaven, which symbolizes the God's residence. It seems that the universe and human world have some coincidence. People cannot help sighing with all sorts of emotions.

The Nine-Dragon Juniper on at northwest side of the Echo Wall. Its trunk is very thick. The trunk is so uneven that it looks like that there are nine dragons circling around it. Therefore, it is called the Nine-Dragon Juniper. It is a primeval cypress of this garden and now it still has luxuriant foliage and spreading branches.

问天柏
Wentan Cypress

古柏参观完圜丘坛的古建筑群,再来看看坛内的古树,有几株树形奇特的古柏让人引发无限联想。回音壁外西南侧有古柏,人称"问天柏",树梢上有一枝丫直指天空,仿佛一人峨冠博带,那高昂的头颅,飘动的衣衫,直向青天的有力的手臂,似满怀悲愤的屈原在质问苍天:"天啊,你享有人间无限敬仰,可曾为人间扫除不平?"它生长在象征上帝的居所皇穹宇院墙外,仿佛自然的造化与人世间有某种契合,让人无限感慨。

九龙柏位于回音壁外西北面,树干粗大,树身凹凸沟回,宛如九龙盘旋,扭结缠绕,森然欲动,故称"九龙柏",九龙柏是园中的原始柏,现在仍枝叶繁茂。

九龙柏
Nine –Dragen Juniper

65

四、与天通声息——祈年殿

Keep Contact with the Sky:
the Hall of Prayer for Good Harvests

祈谷坛的主体建筑祈年殿
The Hall of Prayer for Good Harvests Is the
Main Building of the Altar of Prayer for Good Harvests

　　祈年殿是北京的象征建筑之一，也是世界上最著名的神殿，它的卓越不仅在于其精巧的建筑设计，更在于其建筑构造体现了中国古代哲学思想和天文认识。

The Hall of Prayer for Good Harvests is one of Beijing symbolic constructions, and is also the most famous temple in the world. Its excellence does not only lie in its exquisite design, but also attributes to the fact that its constructional structure represents ancient Chinese philosophy and astronomic knowledge.

1. Red Stairway Bridge

Walking northward from Chenzhen Gate (*Chenzhenmen*), one shall reach the Altar of Prayer for Grain. Here the view suddenly clears up with the high sky and broad earth. This thoroughfare is called "Red Stairway Bridge"(Danbi Bridge), an axis line linking the two great buildings in the south and north of the Temple of Heaven. It is 300-odd meters in length, with the northern end two meters higher than the southern end, the arrangement and design of which show unusual ingenuity. To the south of the axis line is the open, broad, low and level Circular Mound; to the north is the grand and lofty Hall of Prayer for Good Harvest. The Hall of Prayer for Good Harvests is 38 meters high with a triple-eaved roof and three tiers of lofty bases. The Circular Mound is 6 meters high with three tiers of terraces. However, the Imperial Vault of Heaven between the two altars is 19 meters high with a single-eaved roof and lofty bases, which modulates the huge difference in height and obtains the best overall special mix. The Red Stairway Bridge connects the two buildings organically and gradually from the low to the high. The circular enclosed wall of the Imperial Vault of Heaven and the semicircular wall in the north of Echo Wall are strokes of genius in particular. Located in the center of the semicircular wall, Chenzhen Gate is connected with Red Stairway Bridge in the north and Circular Mound Altar in the south, which makes this connection appear less unnatural and abrupt. The Circular Mound and the Hall of Prayer for Good Harvests thus integrate into a perfect whole. Standing at the southern end of Red Stairway Bridge and looking over the Hall of Prayer for Good Harvests, one may feel the amazing grandeur of the lofty and resplendent temple that stands at the end of the road. Struck by the insignificance of oneself, one may even desire to get close to the holy temple and sublimate one's soul. Setting foot on the sacred road and climbing to the height, one may find the trees along the sides gradually become short and small, with the palaces in the distance shining in the light. The sublime atmosphere created by the buildings and trees may be hailed as the acme of perfection.

1. 丹陛桥

　　北出成贞门，就进入了祈谷坛，踏上海墁大道，顿时天高地阔，豁然开朗。这条大道俗称"丹陛桥"，是连接天坛南北两座伟大建筑的轴线，长300多米，北端较南端高出2米多，这种布局设计独具匠心。轴线南部是开阔低缓的圜丘坛，轴线北端是宏伟高大的祈年殿；祈年殿高38米，三重檐，三崇基，圜丘台高6米，三层台面，高低悬殊，但两坛之间的皇穹宇高19米，单檐崇基，使这种高度差异得到谐调，并获得最佳的整体空间组合，丹陛桥由低渐将两组建筑有机地结合起来，特别是皇穹宇的圆形围墙、回音壁北边的半弧形围墙更是神来之笔，成贞门位于弧形墙正中，北接丹陛桥，南连圜丘坛，使得这种结合不显得生硬突兀，圜丘坛和祈年殿达到完美统一。站在丹陛桥南端望祈年殿，气势摄人心魄，神殿巍峨壮美，金碧辉煌，伫立在长路尽头，顿感自身渺小，渴望走近那神圣宫殿，渴望灵魂得到升华。踏上神路，渐次登高，两侧树木渐变矮小，唯有远处宫殿在天光下熠熠生辉，由建筑及植物营造的崇高氛围令人叹为观止。

丹陛桥，一条通天的海墁大道
The Red Stairway Bridge,
A Thoroughfare Connecting with the Sky

圆形建筑,方形壝墙,是"天地方圆"的具体体现
The Circular Buildings and Rectangular Walls Represent the Ancient Chinese Thought-"The Heaven Is Round and the Earth Is Square"

2. Dressing Terrace

To the east of the northern end of Red Stairway Bridge, a square brick terrace is located in the east while facing the west. It is surrounded by white marble balustrade in the north, east and south. This is the so-called Dressing Terrace(*Jufutai*). To the south of the Circular Mound Terrace, there is also a Dressing Terrace, only that it has no white marble balustrade. At the time of sacrifice, a tent is put up on it. The ritual of praying for good harvest is held on the 15th day of the first lunar month, which is after the spring beginnings. It is still rather cold. Besides, the ceremony is performed at the seventh ke (unit of time used in ancient times) before sunrise, which makes it even colder. Several charcoal basins, with lamps lit for illumination are set inside the tent. There are also a warm bed, toilet articles and a dragon-chair, thus gaining the name "small imperial palace." It serves as the change room for the emperor where he puts on the blue sacrificial garment with the yellow imperial rope symbolizing imperial power covered inside, waiting for the moment of the sacrificial ceremony.

3. The Altar of Prayer for Grain

The Altar of Prayer for Grain(*Qigutan*) is the altar for performing the ceremony of praying for good harvest. Being a square brick city, it lies in the northeast of the

具服台,祭祀时皇帝在此更衣
Dressing Terrace, the
Change Room for the
Emperor during the Sacrifice

琉璃门
Glazed Gates

2. 具服台

　　丹陛桥靠近北端东侧,有一方形砖台,坐东朝西,北东南三面围以汉白玉石栏,这就是具服台。圜丘台南同样位置也有具服台,只是没有汉白玉石栏。祭祀时搭有幄帐,祈谷典礼在每年的正月上辛日,虽在立春之后,仍是寒冷之季,祭典在日出前七刻举行,寒冷更增几分,幄帐内设炭盆数个,插灯照明,有暖床、盥洗用品、龙椅,人称"小金殿",皇帝在此更衣,将象征皇权的褚黄龙袍罩在蓝色祭服下,等待祭祀时刻的来临。

3. 祈谷坛

　　祈谷坛是举行祈谷大典的祭坛,位于内坛东北部,是一座方形砖城,有高约4.5米的巨大砖石坛基。方形墙砖砌墙身,墙顶为绿琉璃筒瓦通脊,东西南三面各有三间拱券式砖砌门,均为绿琉璃筒瓦覆盖,南砖门庑殿顶,东西砖门为歇山顶,北面有琉璃门三座,歇山顶蓝琉璃筒瓦,门北即皇乾殿。祈谷坛的中心建筑是祈年殿,还有祈年门、东西配庑、燔柴炉、瘗坎等建筑,附属建筑有长廊、神厨、宰牲亭等。

　　从丹陛桥北行即进入祈谷坛南砖门,这座砖门除中间拱券稍大外,东西拱券大小并不相同,东侧略大,正对着御道,西侧略小,正对着王道,中间神道不可僭越。从南砖门穿过,就看见一座殿宇式的大门,这就是祈年门。

祈年殿夜景 *The Night Scene of the Hall of Prayer for Good Harvests*

inner altar and has a 4.5 meters high base made of brick and stone. The square wall is built by laying bricks with the top ridge made of green glazed pantiles. There are three arched brick gates in the east, west and south, all of which are covered with green glazed pantiles. The south gate has a side-hall roof; the east and west ones have *Xieshan* roof; there are three glazed gates in the north with *Xieshan* roof (a kind of roof) and blue glazed pantiles to the north of which is the Imperial Hall of Heaven (*Huangqiandian*). The central constructions are the Hall of Prayer for Good Harvests, the Gate of Prayer for Good Harvestss, the east and north side halls, Firewood Stove and Yi kan (The Place for Burying the Sacrifice's Hair and Blood). The outbuildings include Long Corridor, Heaven's Kitchen and the Butcher House.

Walking northward from the Red Stairway Bridge, one may enter the Southern Brick Gate of the Altar of Prayer for Grain. The central arch of the gate is slightly larger and the east and west arches are not of the same size. The east one is larger and faces the Imperial Road(*yulu*); the west one is smaller and faces the King Road (*wanglu*). One is not allowed to walk on the Sacred Way in the middle. Walking across the Southern Brick Gate, one may see a large gate in the shape of a temple, the Gate of Prayer for Good Harvests.

4. The Gate of Prayer for Good Harvests

The Gate of Prayer for Good Harvests(*Qinianmen*) has five chambers in width and serves as the ceremonial gate of the Altar of Prayer for Grain. It has a blue glazed side-hall roof, with *danqiaodanang wucaidougong* (a system of brackets in Chinese) and color paintings of "dragon and phoenix embrace the seal". Being

透过祈年门，眺望祈年殿
Watching the Hall of Prayer for Good Harvests from the Gate of Prayer for Good Harvests

4. 祈年门

祈年门面阔五间，为祈谷坛仪门，蓝琉璃庑殿顶，施以单翘单昂五彩斗拱，龙凤和玺彩画，金碧辉煌，庄重典雅，是天坛现存少数明式建筑之一。明间脊枋悬金龙透雕华带匾，青底金书"祈年门"。

resplendent, stately and elegant, it is one of the few existent constructions in the style of Ming dynasty. On the beam of the open chamber is hung a plaque engraved with golden dragons with the gilded inscription "The Gate of Prayer for Good Harvests" against blue settings.

Watching the Hall of Prayer for Good Harvests while standing inside the gate, one may see a grand splendid hall set off by three layers of white marble balustrades. The three layers of azure blue eaves and the golden roof represent the limitless power going upwards.

5. The Hall of Prayer for Good Harvests

Throughout the whole altar the hall is high above and the altar is far below. The hall refers to the Hall of Prayer for Good Harvests and the altar refers to the three-layered white marble round altar. The altar is about 5.2 meters in height. The

高耸入云的祈年殿
The Soaring Hall of Prayer for Good Harvests

　　站在祈年门内端详祈年殿，三层洁白的汉白玉围栏，托出一座端庄壮丽的大殿，三层湛蓝的屋檐，金色的宝顶，显示了向上的无穷力量。

5. 祈年殿

　　整座祭坛上屋下坛，屋即祈年殿，坛即三层汉白玉圆台，坛高约5.2米，上层径约68米，中层径约80米，下层径约91米，各层皆绕以石栏，上层石栏望柱饰以

diameter of the top layer is about 68 meters; the middle layer 80 meters; the bottom layer about 91 meters. Each layer is surrounded by marble balustrade. The balustrade surrounding the top layer is adorned with a spiral dragon with its head emerging from the water face; the balustrade surrounding the middle layer has columns decorated with the painting of a phoenix's head emerging from the water surface; the columns of the bottom layer is adorned with patterns of clouds coming out of the water surface. Along the south–north direction there are three huge white marble red steps with stone carvings. The top tier is engraved with patterns of dragon, the middle tier with patterns of phoenix, and the bottom tier with patterns of mountain, sea and clouds. The stone carvings are exquisite, artistic treasures.

The Hall of Prayer for Good Harvests is 32 meters in height. It has a triple–eaved cone roof made of blue glazes. In the south of the upper eave, a nine–dragon belt golden plaque is hung with the gilded inscription "the Hall of Prayer for Good Harvests" against blue settings. The diameter of the hall is 32.6 meters and stepping into the resplendent, splendid and magnificent hall, one may feel staying in the palaces of heaven. The four Longjing columns (a kind of columns in ancient Chinese architecture) in the middle of the hall are decorated with patterns of lotuses, representing the seasons. The 12 golden columns in the middle layer represent the 12 months and the 12 columns in the outer layer are columns under the eave, which

祈年殿汉白玉雕出水——龙
The White Marble Carving of the Hall of Prayer for Good Harvests–Dragon

祈年殿汉白玉石雕丹陛——凤
The White Marble Red Steps with Stone Carvings in the Hall of Prayer for Good Harvests—Phoenix

祈年殿汉白玉石雕丹陛——云
The White Marble Red Steps with Stone Carvings in the Hall of Prayer for Good Harvests—Clouds

祈年殿汉白玉石雕丹陛——龙
The White Marble Red Steps with Stone Carvings in the Hall of Prayer for Good Harvests–Dragon

祈年殿汉白玉雕出水——云
The White Marble Carving of the Hall of Prayer for Good Harvests—Clouds

祈年殿汉白玉雕出水——凤
The White Marble Carving of the Hall of Prayer for Good Harvests–Phoenix

盘龙，螭首出水；中层望柱饰以凤纹，凤首出水；下层望柱饰以朵云，云纹出水。南北向中陛间有三帧巨大的汉白玉石雕丹陛，上层龙纹，中层凤纹，下层山海云纹，雕刻精美，堪称石刻艺术珍品。

stand for the 12 two-hour intervals in a complete day. The 24 pillars altogether represent the 24 solar terms. The 24 columns and the 4 in the middle symbolize the 28 constellations.(Which form a contrast with the 72 constellations in the Long Corridor). This kind of design represents the ancient Chinese thought of "focus on agriculture"

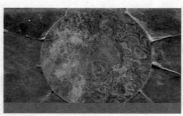

龙凤石
The Stone of Dragon and Phoenix

There are color paintings of dragon and phoenix embracing royal seal inside the Hall of Prayer for Good Harvests. With the golden dragons and the colorful phoenix fluttering, the paintings appear elegant, stately and magnificent. The roof of the hall is in the style of dragon and phoenix algae well. The three layers of the roof of the hall are all round and each contracts gradually, piles up to form a cove. The sculptural decoration of golden dragon and phoenix, their highly protruding heads, the vivid dragon body and phoenix feathers set off the sublimity and grandeur of the heaven with intense decorative effects. In the center of the ground there is a huge round marble, the Stone of Dragon and Phoenix, which is naturally engraved with ink patterns of dragon and phoenix. The dark patterns of the dragon have horn, beard, claw, and tail completely. The patterns of the phoenix are of light color, the feather, head, tail of which are looming and vivid. It responds to the patterns on the algae well in the hall, forming a natural interest. Nine layers of green marbles are laid around the Stone of Dragon and Phoenix.

To the north of the stone is a pedestal of Buddha's statue surrounded by cinnabar balustrade. There are three flights of steps in the south and each flight has five steps. The God of Heaven is enshrined on the pedestal. The tablets of the emperors' ancestors, namely, the gods accompanying the sacrifice, are placed on the lower stone platforms on the right and left of the pedestal. In front of every tablet there is a *biaodou* (bamboo articles used for sacrifices or banquet) table on which sacrificial vessels are displayed. The various offerings sacrificed to the gods are placed in these vessels.

祈年殿内木榫结构 The Wood Tenon Structure of the Hall of Prayer for Good Harvests

The sacrificial vessels of Ming dynasty are porcelain plates and bowels of various colors without fixed colors. During Jingtai period, porcelain Jue (an ancient wine vessel with three legs and a loop handle) was once replaced by jades. In the ninth year of Jaiqing's reign, when the sacrificial ceremony was hold in four suburban areas, the sacrificial vessels used in the four altars were also prescribed. The vessels should comply with the prescribed color and from then on, the vessels used in the Circular Mound Altar have been blue while the patterns of vessels are still plates and calyxes.

At the beginning of Qing dynasty, the system of rituals of Ming dynasty continued to be used. The vessels used in the suburban sacrificial ceremonies were still porcelain plates and bowels. During Yongzheng's reign, the vessels were once changed into cast bronze. The rules were modified during Qianlong's reign. In the 13th year of Qianlong's reign (1748), when sacrifices were offered on the Circular Mound, brand-new vessels were displayed. It was until this period that the vessels achieved the most mature and orderly stage and were kept to by the later generations. Although the scene people can have a view of in the Hall of Prayer for Good Harvests is the original one during Emperor Xianfeng's reign, Emperor Qianlong established the regulations concerning the vessels.

There are a variety of vessels displayed in the Temple of Heaven. They are in different patterns strictly defined. The materials of the vessels are pottery, porcelain, bamboo, timber, gold, silver, jade, gourd, etc. The vessels are also divided into main position, accompanying position and following position according to the rank. They can be used as container, drinking vessel, and eating vessel. The vessels used when praying for good harvest on the Circular Mound are also used in sacrificial ceremonies. However, the vessels in the Altar of Prayer for Grain are of smaller size and are all azure.

In the front of the tablets inside the Hall of Prayer for Good Harvests is displayed a connecting table. On the table are displayed jade, silk and incense.

"Cangbi" has been regarded as of primary importance among the offerings, while the animals, wines and grains are of secondary importance. Cangbi refers to blue round jades. According to the annotation in *Zhou Li* (a classical book in ancient China), "The offerings sacrificed to god must resemble the god. The roundness symbolizes the shape of the sky. Cang is the color of the sky, therefore cang is

祈年殿殿高32米，蓝色琉璃圆形三重檐攒尖顶，上重檐下南向悬挂九龙华带金匾，匾上青底金书"祈年殿"。殿径32.6米，步入大殿，金碧辉煌，富丽庄重，仿佛置身天上宫阙，大殿当中4根龙井柱，柱身饰以沥粉贴金海水江涯西蕃莲纹，象征春夏秋冬四季；中层12根金柱，象征一年的12个月；外层12根为檐柱，象征一天12个时辰；中外两层共24根柱子，象征24个节气，加上中间4根

龙凤藻井 *Dragon and Phoenix Algae Well*

大柱共28根，象征周天二十八星宿。加上柱顶的8根童柱共36根，象征三十六天罡（与长廊七十二地煞相对）。祈年殿的这种设计，是古人"重农"思想的反映。

祈年殿殿内龙凤和玺彩画，金龙飞舞，彩凤翩翩，典雅庄重，富丽堂皇。殿顶为龙凤藻井，上中下三层皆为圆形，层层收缩，叠落起来形成穹隆，斗拱凭榫卯支于圆穹内壁，正中金色龙凤雕饰，高高突起的龙头和凤首，栩栩如生的龙身和凤羽，衬托出天宇的崇高伟大，具有极强的装饰效果。大殿地面中心为一圆形大理石，石上墨色纹理天然勾画出龙凤图案，龙纹色深，角、须、爪、尾俱全，凤纹色浅，羽毛、头、尾隐约可见，惟妙惟肖，人称"龙凤石"。与大殿藻井上的龙凤遥相呼应，天然成趣。殿内环龙凤石铺墁9重艾叶青石。

龙凤石北设有石须弥座，环以朱栏，南向设三出陛，每陛出阶5级。石座上供奉皇天上帝神主，石座左右又设石坪，较石座低，上面供奉陪祀神主即皇帝列祖列宗的神位。每个神位前皆设笾豆案，案上陈列祭器，器内盛放敬献神主的各类供品。

明代的祭器未定其色，形以瓷盘瓷碗为器。景泰年间也曾把瓷爵易之以玉。嘉靖九年（1530年）在四郊分祀的同时，也规定了四郊坛所使用的祭器，要"各依其色"，从此时起圜丘坛祭器为青色，而祭器式样未变，依然为盘盂之属。

清初一切礼仪率依明制，郊祀所用祭器也以瓷盘瓷碗代之，相沿未改。雍正时曾改范铜为器。至清乾隆朝改制，乾隆十三年（1748年）圜丘大祀时陈列了全

明永乐大盘
A Yongle Big Plate of Ming Dynasty

used." (From the chapter named "*Chunguan, dazongbo*". Close to the color of sky, Cangbi is offered to "the God of Heaven" in winter solstice. This vividly reflects an ancient Chinese thought– "The heaven is round and the earth is square" When performing worship to god, the emperor would place Cangbi on a piece of silk, put them into a round bamboo basket and offer them to the god.

配位陈设
The Furnishings in the Accompanying Position

The special silk used in sacrifice is made to order by the government. Silk threads are woven into characters on the exquisitely embroidered silk. The silk is divided into several types according to the rank of the gods worshipped. In Ming dynasty, there were five types of silk, the color of which was determined by the orientation of the objects worshipped. (They were of six colors: dark green, white, blue, yellow, red and black.) In Qing dynasty, Manchu invaded and became the ruler of the Central Plains, therefore the silk in use had its own characteristics– there were both Manchu and Chinese characters on the silk. There were different types of silk used in suburban sacrifice, report sacrifice, ancestor worship sacrifice, god worship sacrifice, achievements report sacrifice, together with white silk sacrifice. The former four types were used in the Temple of Heaven. 12 pieces of azure silk for suburban sacrifice were used in the main position on the Circular Mound; white pieces of silk for ancestor worship were used in the accompanying position; 19 pieces of blue, red, yellow, white and black silk for god worship were used in the following position. Besides, when great events happened, the emperor needed to perform the ceremony of report on the Circular Mound, and several pieces of report sacrifice silk would be used. There are no following positions in the Hall of Prayer for Good Harvests; so only silks for suburban sacrifice and ancestor worship are displayed in it. As for the incenses, there are

新祭器,至此祭器陈设达到最完备规整的阶段,而为后代所遵循。现在人们在祈年殿里看到的场面,虽是咸丰朝祭天时的原貌,但其祭器规制则是乾隆帝亲自制定的。

天坛陈设祭器种类繁多,式样各异,规制严格。从质料上讲有陶、瓷、竹、木、金、银、玉、匏等;按用途分有容器、酒器、食器等;从等级上有正位、配位、从位之分。圜丘、祈谷坛祭器虽都为大祀之用,但祈谷坛祭器尺寸相对较小,颜色均为天青色。

祈年殿内神位前设接桌,接桌上陈玉、帛、香三种物品。

祭天礼仪历来是将"苍璧"列为祭品的首位,其次才是牲牢、酒醴、黍、稷、稻、粱等。青色的圆形玉称为"苍璧"。《周礼·春官·大宗伯》注:"礼神者必象其类,璧圆象天,疏苍元皆是天色,故用苍也。"苍璧取其颜色近于天,因而冬至日祀"皇天上帝"以苍璧,这是中国古代"天圆地方"自然观的生动体现。举行祭天礼仪时由皇帝本人将苍璧放在帛之上,同装在一个篚盒之内,然后上供。

祭祀专用的制帛是由官方定制而成的,绣制精美,用丝线织字于帛上。按祭

竹制的篚有大小两种,分别盛放"郊祀制帛"、"奉先制帛"
Two Kinds of Bamboo Baskets with Different Size.
The Silk Used in Suburban Sacrifice and Ancestor
Worship Sacrifice Are Respectively
Put into the Two Baskets

葫芦形壶,仪程"进俎浇汤"时使用
A Pot in the Shape of a Calabash
Which Is Used in the
Course of Jinzujiaotang

帛
Silk

香盒
Fragrant Cases

瓷爵,为圜丘奉献用,内盛酒,仅用于从位
Jue, for Sacrifice on the Circular Mound.
It Has Wine in It and Can Only
Be Used in the Following Position

83

Miaojinlongzhu and Chenxiangkuai (two kinds of incenses) placed in exquisite incense cases.

6. The East Annex Hall and West Annex Hall

There are the eastern and western buildings outside the Hall of Prayer for Good Harvests. The East Annex Hall and West Annex Hall have nine chambers in the width and the Xieshan roof made of blue glazed pantiles. In early Ming dynasty, when it was still called the Temple of Heaven and Earth, there were nine side buildings in the front and seven at the back. During the reign of Emperor Qianlong, the seven at the back were demolished and there is no trace of them nowadays. The East Annex Hall and West Annex Hall are built on the terrace made of brick and stone. Surrounding the brick terrace, there are stone troughs for draining water. The front eave decorated with windows and doors having partition boards protrudes out of the corridor. In the frontispiece of the open room and to the south and north of the front corridor are nine chuidaitaduo steps (a kind of steps). The wall is painted red based on green bricks, Nowadays East Annex Hall is for music and dancing while the West Annex Hall is the for holding ceremonies.

The eastern building outside the Hall of Prayer for Good Harvests has been turned into a history and culture museum, the exhibition contains four parts including the Hall of Prayer for Good Harvests' History, art of architectural, historical restoration and related events. It shows the history of the Hall of Prayer for Good Harvests during three periods by introducing the Hall of Great Sacrifice, the Hall of Great Enjoyment and the Hall of Prayer for Good Harvests. The exhibition introduces and analies the construction technology of the Hall of Prayer for Good Harvests by building models, historical materials, photographs and through building implication, spar frame structure, cornerstone carving etc.The Hall of Prayer for Good Harvests is concerned to some major event in the China's history, and the building itself has a major impact on history too. The exhibition introduces the Jiajing restructuring, the big fire the Hall of Prayer for Good Harvest, "Constitution of the Temple of Heaven," and so on. The Hall of Prayer for Good Harvests experienced three heavy repairs separately in 1935, 1971 and 2005; the exhibition shows the relevant materials and photos, more detailedly introduces the cases of the

祈年殿东配殿 *The East Annex Hall of the Hall of Prayer for Good Harvests*

祀对象不同等级，其制帛又区别为若干种。明代制帛分五等，以祭祀对象之方位定有六种颜色：苍、白、青、黄、赤、黑。清王朝因是满族入主中原，所以使用制帛又有其特点，即在制帛上绣织有满汉两种文字。各色制帛计有郊祀制帛、告祀制帛、奉先制帛、礼神制帛、展亲制帛、报功制帛以及素帛，前四种制帛为天坛祭天之用。圜丘正位用天青色"郊祀制帛"十二端；配位用白色"奉先制帛"，随配位数定；从位用青、赤、黄、白、黑各色"礼神制帛"十九端，各依其方色。此外，如国家遇有大事需在圜丘行告祀礼时，天坛又用"告祀制帛"数端。现祈年殿内因无从位，只陈设郊祀制帛和奉先制帛。香则有描金龙柱香，沉香块等，都陈放在精美的香盒里。

6. 祈年殿东西配殿

出祈年殿，东西配庑面阔九间，蓝色琉璃筒瓦歇山式殿顶。明初的天地坛，配庑为前后两重，前九间后七间，清乾隆时撤后重七间，今已无痕迹。祈年殿东西配庑建于砖石台基之上，环砖基有排水石槽，前檐出廊，装修为隔扇门窗，明间正面及前廊南北各有垂带踏跺9级，墙身涂朱，下肩青砖。

祈年殿东配殿现已辟为祈年殿历史文化展馆，展览内容为祈年殿历史沿革、建筑艺术、历次修缮、相关重大事件等四部分。通过介绍大祀殿、大享殿、祈年殿三个时期来展示祈年殿的历史脉络。展览采用建筑模型、史料、图片等形式从建筑寓意、梁架结构、崇基石雕几个方面剖析介绍了祈年殿的建筑工艺。祈年殿

东配殿
The East Annex Hall

three heavy repairs.

The Hall of Prayer for Good Harvests is recognized as the wooden structure architectural masterpiece all over the world, and has a high historical and scientific value. The building implicates the Chinese traditional of the universe and other philosophical concepts, the building structure and techniques reflect the wooden structure of ancient Chinese architecture, represent the highest level of the Chinese ancient architecture. The visitors can feel the strong historical atmosphere, gust heaven Charm of Chinese ancient worship culture of heaven Charm.

The western building outside the Hall of Prayer has been turned into a worship of heaven museum, shows the whole process of ritual worship of heaven to the visitors. Temple of Heaven cultural studies have summarized into a cumbersome process of the worship of heaven, and have detailed introduced from the taking preparation before sacrificing, to display two days before the festival, to the emperor how to salute. There are a large picture which painted a large number of worship teams and the quality of ritual artifacts which collected in the Temple of Heaven, including the soft spun gold light, scent stove, porcelain beans, such as clothing, and other precious relics.

与中国历史上一些重大事件有着极大的关联，其建筑本身也曾在历史上有着重大影响，展览还介绍了嘉靖改制、祈年殿火灾、"天坛宪法"等事件。近现代祈年殿经历了1935年、1971年、2005年三次大修，展览展出了相关资料、照片，较详细地介绍了三次大修的情况。

祈年殿是世界公认的木构建筑杰作，具有极高的历史价值和科学价值。祈年殿建筑寓意了中国传统的宇宙观及其他哲学观念，祈年殿的建筑结构、工艺集中了中国古代木结构建筑之大成，代表了中国古代建筑工艺的最高水平。游客在这里可以感受到浓厚的历史氛围，领略中国的古代祭天文化的神韵。

祈年殿西配庑现辟为祭天礼仪馆，向游人展示了祭天礼仪的整个过程。天坛文化研究人员将繁琐祭天过程归纳成项，从祭祀前请示筹备，到祭礼前两天陈

祭天礼仪馆内景
The Inner Sight of the Hall for Holding Ceremonie

7. The Imperial Heaven Hall

Walking northward round the Hall of Prayer for Good Harvests, one may see the courtyard of the Imperial Heaven Hall(*Huangqiandian*). The Imperial Heaven Hall is where the tablets of god are stored. On the day of the ceremony of grain prayers, the tablets of god are carried to the Hall of Prayer for Good Harvests to be worshipped, while at other times, they will be worshipped in the Imperial Heaven Hall. Every first and fifth day of the lunar month, the officials of Ministry of Rites and Taichang Temple would sweep and burn the incense.

The Imperial Heaven Hall has five chambers in the width, with the red steps in front of the hall enclosed by white marble balustrade. To the south there are three flights of steps and to the east and west there is one flight of steps. All of the flights have eight steps. A nine-dragon belt plaque with the gilded inscription "the Imperial Heaven Hall" is hung under the eave, which comes from the Ming Shizong Emperor Zhu Houcong. On the stone pedestal of Buddha's statue in the frontispiece a shrine is placed, in which the tablet of the god of heaven is enshrined. Behind the tablet there is a folding screen engraved with patterns of draon Patterns. Along its two sides, the shrine of the emperor's ancestors is displayed. An incense burner table is set in front of the tablets of god, on which five offerings are displayed. On the day before the sacrifice, the emperor would go to the Imperial Heaven Hall, burn joss sticks and perform worship.

The Imperial Heaven Hall is a separate courtyard. The glazed gate in the northern wall of the Altar of Prayer for Grain is the gate of the Imperial Heaven Hall. There

皇乾殿内陈设
The Displays in the Imperial Hall of Heaven

皇乾殿
The Imperial Hall of Heaven

设,再到皇帝如何行礼都有详细介绍。内有描绘人数众多的祭祀队伍的大型图画,陈列了天坛所藏祭祀文物精品,其中有祭祀时陈设的软金丝灯、金熏炉、祭蓝釉瓷、瓷豆及服饰等珍贵文物。

7. 皇乾殿

绕过祈年殿向北,就是皇乾殿院落。皇乾殿是存放祈谷神位的场所,举行祈谷大典当日,神位被龙亭抬至祈年殿供奉外,其余日子则在皇乾殿供奉,每月的朔望之日(即初一、十五)由礼部及太常寺官员洒扫上香。

皇乾殿五开间,殿前丹墀为汉白玉石栏,南向三出陛,东西各一出陛,俱八级,檐下悬九龙华带匾,匾上青地金书"皇乾殿",为明世宗朱厚熜亲题。殿内正面石须弥座,上有神龛,龛内供奉"皇天上帝"神位,神位后护雕龙屏风,两侧亦有石台,供奉皇帝列祖列宗神龛,神位前设香案,上陈五供。祭祀前一日,皇帝亲自到皇乾殿拈香行礼。

is another gate outside the western wall of the Imperial Heaven Hall, the famous "Seventy-Year-Old Door". We should begin with the "Sixty-Year-Old Door" as we mention "Seventy-Year-Old Door".

8. Sixty-Year-Old Door and Seventy-Year-Old Door

Every year, the day before the ceremony, the emperor would enter the Gate of Altar of Prayer for Grain (today's West Gate), proceed pass the Western Gate of Heaven to the Red Stairway Bridge. He would descend the imperial carriage, walk to the Southern Brick Gate of the Altar of Prayer for Grain, then pass the Gate of Prayers for Good Harvest to the Imperial Heaven Hall and perform worship in these places. Then he would walk out of Western Brick Gate, lodge in the Palace of Abstinence, waiting for the moment of sacrifice piously and serenely. On the day of sacrifice, the emperor would set out from the Palace of Abstinence, ride on the ceremonial chariot to the western end in the south of the Red Stairway Bridge, then walk to the altar to hold the ceremony. The emperor who serves the main role in the sacrifice feels very tired in every sacrifice. In the 37th year of Qianlong's reign, (1772), Emperor Qianlong was 62 years old, more than sixty years old. The complex rituals make him greatly tired in body and mind. Therefore, another gate was added in the Southern Brick Gate, the "Sixty-Year-Old Door" (*Huajia Door*)and the rules were also changed to the effect that instead of walking across the Red Stairway Bridge, the emperor could directly reach the altar from the "Sixty-Year-Old Door" thus saving a lot of walking. However, Emperor Qianlong paid strong veneration to the Supreme Being throughout his life and gave orders that "after ascending the throne, the emperor should not neglect to worship heaven. Those who have not reached 60 years old are not allowed to walk across the gate, which is a decree forever." He also decreed that "only those who have reached 70 years old can walk across the "Seventy-Year-Old Door" *Guxi* Door." Most of the emperors of later generations did not live longer than their great ancestor. Only Emperor Jiaqing once passed through the "Sixty-Year-Old Door" while no one had the luck to pass through the "Seventy-Year-Old Door".

花甲门
Sixty-Year-Old Door

　　皇乾殿是一单独院落,祈谷坛北墙上的琉璃门即为皇乾殿院门,皇乾殿西墙外亦有一院门,即有名的"古稀门",提起"古稀门",还要从"花甲门"说起。

8. 花甲门、古稀门

　　每年祈谷大典前一日,皇帝入祈谷坛门(今天坛西门),经西天门至丹陛桥西侧降辇,然后步行至祈谷坛南砖门,经过祈年门至皇乾殿等处行礼,然后皇帝出西砖门,宿天坛斋宫,虔心静气等待祭祀时刻。祭祀当日,皇帝再从斋宫出发,乘礼舆至丹陛桥南端西侧,步行至祭坛行礼,作为祭典主要角色的皇帝每次行礼都十分辛苦。乾隆三十七年(1772年),乾隆皇帝62岁,已过花甲之年,繁琐的礼仪使他身心疲惫,于是在祈谷坛南砖门增开一门,即"花甲门",并修改礼仪;皇帝不需走丹陛桥,而直接从花甲门登上祈谷坛,节省了许多步履。乾隆四十六年(1781年)乾隆皇帝年逾古稀,又在皇乾殿西墙外新设一门,被人称作"古稀门"。此门一开,皇帝无须穿过祈谷坛,而直接从皇乾殿西门进入皇乾殿,又节省了许多路途。但乾隆皇帝一生敬天虔诚,下旨告诫子孙,关于花甲门:"即位之后,敬天报本不可疏略,若未满六旬者,不得路经此门,著永远为令",而古稀门更是"有寿登古稀者,方可出入此门",后世皇帝大多没有他们的高祖长寿,仅有嘉庆一人走过花甲门,古稀门则无人幸运通过。

五、宴席之所——
神库、神厨、宰牲亭

The Feasting Place: Divine Storehouse,
Divine Kitchen and the Butcher House

长廊
The Long Corridor

祭祀大典,百密不可一疏,盛装、盛舞,自然也有盛宴。祭器的不厌精细,祭天用的稻谷是人君亲耕而获,祭天用玉帛是皇后亲手养蚕取丝而织,祭天的仪程,环环相接,繁而不乱。

1. 长廊

出祈谷坛东砖门,进入长廊,长廊是通往神厨、宰牲亭的通道。古代礼仪规定,杀牲地点即宰牲亭,应距祭坛二百步以外,为了使供品不被雨雪风沙所污,建有曲尺长廊,联檐通脊。起点为祈谷坛东砖门,中间为神厨,终点即宰牲亭。宰杀后的牲畜通过长廊送往神厨,祭祀当日夜半时,也将神厨制作供品通过长廊送至坛上。

The sacrificial ceremony should be extremely carefully prepared. Besides the splendid attire and dancing, there should also be grand banquets. In addition to the fineness of the sacrificial vessels, the emperor planted the rice and the empress raises silkworms to produce the silk used in the ceremony. The complex procedures of the rituals do not appear confusing for they are linked with each other.

1. The Long Corridor

Walking out of the Eastern Brick Gate of the Altar of Prayer for Grain; one may enter the Long Corridor, which leads to the Divine Kitchen and the Butcher House. According to ancient norms of rites, the place for slaughtering animal sacrifice should be more than 200 steps away from the sacrificial altar. In order to prevent the offerings from being stained by rain, snow, wind or sand, winding corridors are built to connect the eaves and ridges. The starting point is the Eastern Brick Gate of the Altar of Prayer for Grain, with the Divine Kitchen in the middle and the Butcher House in the end. After being slaughtered, the animals are carried to the Divine Kitchen through the Long Corridor. On the day of sacrifice, at midnight, the offerings made in the Divine Kitchen are carried to the altar.

The Long corridor has 72 chambers with green glazed tiles and vermilion columns. Taking blue, green and black as the main colors, the *Yawumoxuanzi* color paintings (a kind of ancient Chinese painting) look natural, simple and fresh. The Long Corridor was originally an enclosed veranda, with grid windows in the front and walls at the back. The lamps would be placed at short intervals to illuminate the corridor. Now with the grid windows removed, the stretches of grassland in the south and age-old cypresses reaching the sky create a bight and open view. A lot of theater fans and amateur performers often get together in the Long Corridor and one can hear the endless sound of gongs, drums, *huqin* (a two stringed bowed instrument). The Beijing accent and dialect attract the travelers to stay and listen, thus making the Long Corridor become a real pleasure veranda.

2. The Seven-Star Stones

The Seven-Star Stones on the grassland in the south of Long Corridor is said to be an aerolite. However, the carved patterns on them make it clear that the stones are

长廊72间，绿琉璃瓦朱红漆柱，蓝绿黑为主要色调的雅伍墨旋子彩画，素淡清爽。长廊原为封闭式廊房，前设槛窗，后为垣墙。使用时，廊内隔不远即设插灯，以备照明。现长廊槛窗拆除，视野开阔，南面大片草地，古柏参天。平日多有戏迷票友聚集长廊，锣鼓胡琴之声不绝于耳，京腔京韵引人驻足，真正成为游廊。

2. 七星石

长廊南侧草地有"七星石"，传说为天上陨石，但石头上人工雕刻花纹，一望而知乃人为放置。七星石按北斗七星形象排列，石上刻山形云朵纹。传说明嘉靖年间改建大享殿时，道士向嘉靖帝进言，称大殿巽方(东南方)空虚无物，不利于皇图永固及国祚绵长，对皇帝的寿命亦十分不利，建议用镇石，嘉靖帝笃信道教，听从道士建议，在此设七星石镇压风水。清入关后，在七星石东北侧又加一石，七星石名虽未改，但实有8块巨石。

placed there by human beings. Engraved with patterns of mountain and clouds, the Seven-Star Stones are displayed according to the shape of Big Dipper. It is said that during the reign of Emperor Jiaqing, when rebuilding the Great Hall for Sacrificial Rituals (*Daxiangdian*), a Taoist said to the emperor that the vacancy in the southeast of the hall went against the stability of imperial rule and the continuity of the national fortunes, and also greatly threaten the emperor's longevity. He advised to use a stone for suppressing. Emperor Jiaqing believed firmly in Taoism and placed the Seven-Star Stones to suppressing geomantic omen. When the Qing troops entered the frontier pass, another stone was added in the northeast of the Seven-Star Stones. The name stays the same but there are actually 8 huge stones. To the north of the Long Corridor is a cypress over 500 years old. The pagoda tree in its arms is also about 100 years old. The two of them embrace each other and become inseparable, thus getting the name "Cypress Embracing Pagoda Tree (*Baibaohuai*)" When spring comes, light green branches and buds stretch from the pagoda tree and set off the dark blue age-old cypress, which creates a special attractive sight.

3. The Divine Storehouse and Divine Kitchen

Getting out of the Altar of Prayer for Grain, walking along the Long Corridor, and turning left, you shall enter a spacious courtyard. The main hall located in the north and facing the south is the Divine Storehouse, while the East Annex Hall and West Annex Hall are the Divine Kitchen. The offerings made in the courtyard of the Divine Kitchen were stored in the Divine Storehouse.

The Divine Storehouse is in the style of *Xuan shan*. It has a roof with green glazed tiles and five chambers in the width. The open chambers have *Luodilinghua* (a kind of pattern) windows with partition board and flights of steps in the front. The other chambers are all based on green bricks and have windows with partition board above. In the Divine Kitchen once a *biandou* (bamboo articles used for sacrifices or banquet) table was placed to perform the ritual of "watching the biandou" which means on the day before the sacrifice, the emperor would go to he Divine Storehouse or sent princes to inspect the biandou and examine the making of offerings.

The Divine Kitchen is the place for making offerings. In the same style of construction

柏抱槐
Cypress Embracing Pagoda Tree

　　长廊北侧有一株柏树,树龄500多年,它怀里的槐树大约也有100多年,两树相拥难以分离,人称"柏抱槐",每至春天,柏树怀里的槐树长出嫩绿枝芽,沧桑古柏和青枝嫩叶相映成趣,成为独特景观,引人驻足。

with the Divine Storehouse, the Divine Kitchen has a Xuan shan roof with green glazed tiles, a Wuhua fastigium, and Xuanzi color paintings. All kinds of kitchen appliances are available, with guotai (the top of a kitchen range) and sinks in it. Now one can find no trace of them.

Inside the Divine Kitchen there is the famous Sweet Spring Well, which is placed in a pavilion with a hexa—angled roof in the shape of a case and green glazed tiles. Being sweet and cold, the water of the well is used to cook the offerings. The well is said to be able to reach the Heaven and therefore is incomparably mellifluent. Inside the courtyard of the Divine Kitchen, the dark and luxuriantly green ancient cypresses appear to be reaching the sky. The bronze cauldrons once used in the sacrifice are still left in the courtyard, from which one can catch a glimpse of the pomp of the ceremony in those years.

At the moment of sacrifice, the divine tables were loaded with sacrificial vessels filled with various foods. They were firstly enshrined in the main hall of the Divine Kitchen. The rich foods, exquisite cooking arts, careful arrangement constituted the main part of the complete and solemn rituals of heaven worship. According to the

北神厨正殿即神库 *The Main Hall in the North of the Divine Kitchen–the Divine Storehouse*

甘泉井
Sweet Spring Well

3. 神库、神厨

出祈谷坛东砖门沿长廊左转即进入一宽敞院落,坐北朝南正殿即为神库,东西配庑即为神厨。神厨院内制作完毕的供品,在神库内放置。

神库为悬山式建筑,绿琉璃瓦顶,面阔五开间,明间落地棱花隔扇窗,前出陛,次稍间皆下肩青砖,上为隔扇窗。当年神厨内设笾豆案,有"视笾豆"的礼仪,即祀前一日皇帝亲自或派遣亲王到神库内阅视笾豆,检查供品制作情况。

神厨是制作供品的场所,神厨内制作完毕的供品,在神库内放置。神厨同神库建筑形式相同,绿琉璃瓦悬山顶五花山墙,旋子彩画,旧时凡是厨房用具一应俱全,内有锅台、涤洗池等,现已无痕迹。神厨内有著名的甘泉井,六角顶亭,绿琉璃瓦,井水甘洌,用来烹制祭天供品,传说井水可达天界,因而甘美无比。

神厨院内有古柏参天,苍翠葱郁,现院内仍有当时祭礼所用铜锅,当年盛况略见一斑。

direction of the altar, biandou table was also placed in the Divine Storehouse. On the table various kinds of sacrificial vessels filled with different foods were displayed in accordance with the order. Deng was in the middle, with fu in the left and gui in the right. The bian followed the fu and the zu was in front of the table.

The *deng* (a kind of vessel) was filled with taigeng, brewis without spices of five flavors. Xing(a kind of vessel) was filled with *hegeng*, the brewis with spices. In the sacrificial ceremony, *taigeng* was higher in rank than hegeng. Fu and *gui* (both are vessels) were filled with different foods. The two fu were filled with *shu* (glutinous millet) and ji, the rice braised from millet. The two *gui* were filled with paddy, and fine grain, which are rice and broomcorn respectively. 12 bian were filled with *xingyan, gaoyu, zao, su, zhen, ling, qing, lufu, baibing, heibing, xiuer, fenci* in order. 12 dou were filled with *jiuzu, qingzu, luhai, jinzu, tuhai, sunzu, yuhai, pixi, tunbo, shi, sanshi* in order. All these offering were cooked on the day before the sacrifice and examined by the doctors from Taichang Temple. Then they were displayed on the

祭天仪程之一 ——"进俎浇汤"
One of the Courses of the Heaven Worshipping Ceremonies—Jinzujiaotang

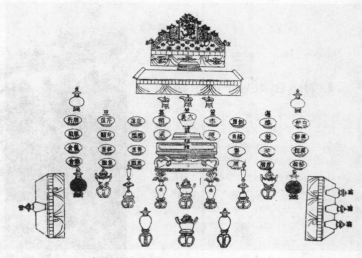

祈谷坛正位陈设图
A View of the Main Position on the Altar of Prayer for Good Harvests

　　祭天之际,盛着各种食物的祭器摆满神案,先供奉在正殿神库内。这些食品之丰盛,制作工艺之精美,陈设铺排之讲究成为祭天礼仪完备和隆重的一个主要内容。神库内也按祭坛的位置设笾豆案。案上排列的各式祭器内盛以不同祭品,并各以其序:簠左簋右,笾从簠,豆从簋,俎在案前。

　　登内实以"太羹",即不加五味作料的纯牛肉汤。铏内实以"和羹",即调和五味的牛肉汤。在祭礼中"太羹"比"和羹"等级更高。簠内食品各不相同,两个中各盛以黍和稷,黍为黄米、黏米饭,稷为小米蒸制的白米饭;两个簋中各盛以稻和粱,分别为大米饭、高粱米饭。笾十二品内各实以一种祭品,按次序为:铏盐、藁鱼、枣、栗、榛、菱、芡、鹿脯、白饼、黑饼、糗饵、粉糍。豆十二品内亦各实以一种祭品,依次为:韭菹、醓醢、菁菹、鹿醢、芹菹、兔醢、笋菹、鱼醢、脾析、豚胉、酏食、糁食。所有这些祭品是在祀前一日,由太常寺博士监视制作,然后依次展器于神库的笾豆案上,等候皇帝前来省视,名为"视笾豆"。

biandou table, waiting for the emperor to inspect.

4. The Butcher House

Getting out of the courtyard of the Divine Kitchen, and walking westward along the Long Corridor, one may enter the courtyard of the Butcher House. Located at the eastern end of the Long Corridor, the Butcher Househas a double-eaved Xieshan roof. It has five chambers in the width and 3 chambers in the depth. There are gates to the east and south of the courtyard. In the west of the marble terrace with red steps, is the southern gate, a gate connected to the Long Corridor by the passage hall. There is also a well pavilion in the courtyard, the same as the one in the Divine Kitchen. The Butcher Houseis also called "the Pavilion for Beating Animal Sacrifice" This is because in the ancient times, the animal sacrifice was beaten with mallets, instead of being butchered with knife.

北宰牲亭
North Butcher House

4. 宰牲亭

　　出了神厨院落沿长廊西行，即进入宰牲亭院，宰牲亭在长廊东尽头，重檐歇山顶大殿，面阔五间，进深三间，院落东向、南向各设门。南向门在大殿丹墀石台西侧，为一过道门，通过过厅即与长廊相连。院中亦有井亭，与神厨内井亭相同。宰牲亭又称"打牲亭"，因古时祭祀牺牲不是用刀屠杀，而是用专用木槌击打而得名。

六、皇家祭天大典乐府——
神乐署

The Official Conservatory of Royal Ceremony
of Heaven Worship:Divine Music Office

凝禧殿,乐舞生演练祭祀乐舞的地方,现门前依然留有站位
The Hall of Gathered Happiness, Where the Dancers Perform the Music and Dancing of Sacrifice. There Are Still Standing Places Left in front of the Door

　　为了祭祀,古人甚至要专设一个艺术学校,培养年轻的歌舞人才,这里便成了森森仪法的音乐殿堂。

　　神乐署在天坛外坛西南,斋宫西侧,坐西朝东,自成一院落。明洪武朝朱元璋在南京郊坛就建有神乐观,永乐皇帝朱棣迁都北京后,仿南京旧制在天地坛西部仍建神乐观,演习祭祀乐舞。

　　神乐署初名神乐观是因为明代皇帝崇尚道教,明代大礼之前百官都要到道教宫观演习有关礼仪。当时神乐观的乐舞官、生均由道士担任,负责培养和训练乐舞人才,"以备大祀天地、神及宗庙社稷之祭",故神乐观又称"天坛道院"。永乐十八年(1420年)迁都时,有300名乐舞生随驾进京,以后明代神乐观常保持有乐舞生600名左右,到嘉靖朝乐舞生总人数达2200名。清乾隆八年(1743年)神乐观改称神乐所,乾隆二十五年(1760年)又改称为神乐署,以后一直沿用。

凝禧殿内悬图，中和韶乐以要"玉振金声"尽显皇家气派
The plaque Hung inside the Hall of Gathered Happines–Gold in the
Sound of Bronze Bronze Bells and Stone in the Sound of Jade and Stone Ohimes

The ancients even found a school of arts to train excellent young singers and dancers for sacrifice. This school thus becomes the hall of music for the solemn rituals.

The Divine Music Office(*Sheng Yueshu*) is in the southwest of the Temple of Heaven's outer part, to the west of the Fasting Palace. Located in the west while facing the east, the Divine Music Office is a courtyard by itself. Emperor Zhu Yuanzhang (the founder and first emperor of Ming Dynasty) built a Divine Music Temple. After moving the capital to Beijing, following the old system used in Nanjing city, Emperor ZhuDi also built a Divine Music Temple in the west of the Temple of Heaven and Earth to practice the music and dancing of sacrifice.

The Divine Music Office was called the Divine Office Temple in early times. This is because Ming emperors advocated Taoist and the officials should go to the Taoist temple or palace to rehearse relative rituals before a ceremony was hold. At that time, the officials and trainees of the Divine Music Temple were all Taoists. They were responsible for cultivating and training excellent singers and dancers to prepare for the rituals of worshipping heaven, earth, gods, ancestors and society. Therefore the Divine Music Temple was also called "the Taoist Temple of the Temple of Heaven". In the 18th year of Zhu di's reign, (1420) the capital was moved to Beijing and 300 singers and dancers followed the emperor to come to Beijing. Since then, the Divine Music Temple usually kept about 600 singers and dancers. The

神乐署正中大殿五间名"太和殿",紫禁城内有太和殿,为避免重名,康熙十二年(1673年)改神乐观"太和殿"为凝禧殿。凝禧殿是乐舞生演礼的大殿,十分宽敞,绿琉璃瓦庑殿顶,五彩斗拱,殿前有宽月台,月台北原竖有明弘治、清康熙修缮神乐署的碑记。殿后是供奉北方镇护神真武大帝的大殿,明初称玄武殿,后改为显佑殿,绿琉璃瓦歇山顶,面阔七间,显佑殿左右各有三间券棚顶式建筑,分别为江东殿和真官殿,供祀道家的仙乐和乐祖。

神乐署署门旧时气势颇大,三间崇基,东向面对祭坛,绿琉璃瓦歇山顶,门前原有巨大影壁,传说端午节摸此壁可以驱五毒,游人纷至沓来,曾盛极一时。天坛虽然是"郊坛重地",但神乐署一带历来熙来攘往,商贩云集。乾隆六年(1741年),皇帝下诏坛庙重地严禁商贾云集,令神乐观内禁止栽花,各种铺面迁至坛外,以净坛地。因屡禁不止,次年又下诏严禁乐官习道教,不愿从业的人削籍为民,神乐观中道士尽遭驱逐,神乐观没有了道士遂改名为神乐所,乐舞生选年少俊秀

宽敞的凝禧殿
The Spacious Hall of Gathered Happiness

number of singers and dancers reached 2,200 during the reign of Emperor Jiaqing. In the 8th year of Qianlong's reign(1743), the Divine Music Temple was changed to Divine Music Place, which was later changed to Divine Music Office in the 25th year of Qianlong's reign(1755)and stayed unchanged from then on.

In the Divine Music Office, the five main halls in the center are called "Hall of Supreme Harmony". To avoiding using the same name with the Hall of Supreme Harmony in the Forbidden City, in the 12th year of Kangxi's reign (1673), it was renamed as "the Hall of Gathered Happiness" It is the hall for singers and dancers to perform the rituals. Being very spacious, the hall has a side hall's roof with green glazed tiles, *wucaidougong* (a system of brackets in Chinese) and broad platforms in the front. In the north of the platform tablets recording how Emperor Hongzhi of Ming dynasty and Emperor Qianlong of Qing dynasty repaired the Divine Music Office were once established. Behind the hall is another hall where Zhenwu Heavenly Emperor (a northern god for suppression and protection) was enshrined. This hall was originally named Xuanwu Hall(*Xuanwudian*), and was changed to Xianyou Hall (*Xianyoudian*) later. Having a a Xieshan roof with green glazed tiles and seven chambers in the width, Xianyou Hall contained three building with a roof in the shape of arched canopy, namely the Jiangdong Hall (*jiangdongdian*) and Zhanguan Hall (*Zhanguandian*) where the celestial music and founder of music in Taoist were enshrined.

The Divine Music Office had a grand air in the past. Facing the sacrificial altar in the east, the hall has three tall bases and a *Xieshan* roof with green glazed tiles. Huge screen walls were once placed in front of the gate. It is said that on the day of dragon boat festival, touching the wall could drive away five poisonous creatures, so the travelers came here in a continuous stream, which became a fashion in a period. Although the Temple of Heaven was "important place of suburban altar", the Divine Music Office was always crowded with people and merchants. In the 6th year of Qianlong's reign (1742), the emperor decreed that merchants were forbidden to swarm in the temple and altar and planting flowers were forbidden in the Divine Music Temple. Various kinds of stores were moved outside to purify the altar. The government's repeated decrees did not take effect. Therefore, Emperor Qianlong gave orders to prohibit the musician officials from believing in Taoist, and the disobedient would be changed into civilians. The Taoists in the temple were all

殿檐上的仙人走兽
The Fairies and Beasts on the Eave of the Hall

dispelled. Without Taoists, the Divine Music Temple was renamed as Divine Music Place. The singers and dancers were selected form young and handsome descendents of the Eight Banners. In early Qing dynasty, the Divine Music Temple served as the most advanced school of music and dancing. The government established special institutions and employed experts to cultivate and train the singers and dancers at any moment. Influenced by traditions, the area of Divine Music Office was still not serene and quiet. In the 13th year of Jiaqing's reign (1808), Emperor Jiaqing decreed for the second time that the stores in the Divine Music Office be shut down except the chemists'.

Although the Divine Music Office was always noisy, the sacrificial music and dancing has been performed with solemnity. The sacrificial music belongs to Ceremonial music(*Yayue*), which comes from the system of ceremonial music in Zhou dynasty, the music of "*jiao, miao*, yan and she" It had no uniformed name originally. It was until the Warring States Period that the music was named Ceremonial music or Ceremonial ode. The Ceremonial music is also called eight sounds music. The instruments are made of eight kinds of materials: gold, stone, silk, bamboo, earth, wood, gourd and leather, so they have the sight sounds completely. In Zhou dynasty, the instruments used to play the Ceremonial music in the suburban temple when holding a

神乐署通脊连房及院内古槐
The Ancient Cypress in the Courtyard of the Divine Music Office

的八旗子弟充任。清初神乐观作为当时最高的乐舞学府,朝廷设立专门机构和专职人员对祭天乐舞生随时进行培养和训练。大约是历来传统所致,神乐署一带仍不清静。直到嘉庆十三年(1808年),嘉庆帝再次下令取缔神乐署内商店,而将诸家药店保留。

神乐署周围环境虽然一直嘈杂喧闹,但演习祭祀乐舞始终严肃进行。祭天

ceremony include *zhu, yu, bofu, bell, qing, jiangu, paixiao, sheng, gan, yun, chi,* and *se* etc. The *zhu, yu* and *bofu* have been used only in playing Ceremonial music since Dongzhou dynasty. Most of the instruments, including the bell and chime stone were also used in playing non-ceremonial court music, while the *sheng, gan, yun, chi, paixiao* and *se* are also popular among the people. Bell, chime stones, jiangu have been used only in playing Ceremonial music since Qinhan dynasty. *Yun, chi, chi, paixiao* and *se* were gradually lost among the people and became exclusively used in playing Ceremonial music. The instruments used in the Ceremonial music in Ming and Qing dynasties became relatively fixed, and most of the instruments were hard to hear in daily life, which were only used in the music and dancing in the rituals of heaven worship.

天坛古乐器——编钟
An Exhibition of the Ancient Musical Instruments in the Temple of Heaven

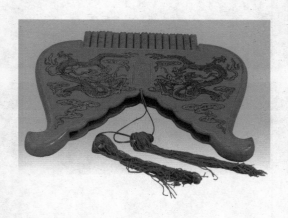

凤尾箫、埙均为中和韶乐演奏乐器
Fengweixiao, Yun, Both Are the Musical Instruments for
Performing Zhongheshaoyue

音乐属雅乐，雅乐源自周代的礼乐制度，"郊、庙、燕、射"之乐，原无统一名称，春秋、战国时才开始被称为"雅乐"或"雅颂"之声。雅乐也称八音乐，乐器使用金、石、丝、竹、土、木、匏、革八种材料制成，因而八音俱全。周代郊庙大典中使用雅乐乐器有柷、敔、搏拊、钟、磬、建鼓、排箫、笙、竽、埙、篪、瑟等，其中的柷、敔、搏拊等件。在东周以后，专用以雅乐，多数乐器，包括钟、磬在内的非礼仪性质的宫廷宴乐中也使用，而笙、竽、埙、篪、排箫、瑟等则在民间也广为流传。秦汉以后，钟、磬、建鼓等成为雅乐专用乐器，埙、篪、排箫、瑟等在民间已渐渐失传，但也成为雅乐的专用乐器。明清雅乐中使用的乐器已经相对固定，多数乐器人们在日常生活中已难得听到，而仅在祭天乐舞时使用。

　　明洪武年间，雅乐改称中和韶乐，去掉了前代的宫悬，规模大为减小，所用乐

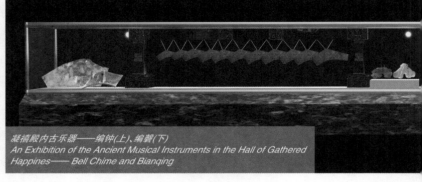

凝禧殿内古乐器——编钟(上)、编磬(下)
An Exhibition of the Ancient Musical Instruments in the Hall of Gathered Happines—— Bell Chime and Bianqing

During Hongwu Period of Ming dynasty, the Ceremonial music was renamed as *Zhongheshaoyue*. Deleting gongxuan of the previous dynasty, the scale diminished greatly. There were only one set of bell and chime stone, both of which contain 16 pieces, 10 qin, 4 se and *bofu*, one zhu and yu, 4 yun, chi and flutes, 8 *xiao* and *sheng*, one *yinggu*, 22 *ge*. An official who are responsible for adjusting the tune led the singers and dancers. 4 *fengsheng,* 2 yun were added later while the *bofu* were reduced to 2. There were dances to praise the achievements in warfare and also dances to praise the achievements in culture. 64 *Wu* dancers held shield and axe and 64 *Wen* dancers held feather fans.They were led by two teachers who.

In Qing dynasty, the system of Ming dynasty was still followed. The Ceremonial

器仅有编钟、编磬各1,每套各16枚,琴10,瑟、搏拊各4,柷、敔各1,埙、篪、笛各4,箫、笙各8,应鼓1,歌22,协律郎1人执麾引领。后又增篪、凤笙各4,埙2,搏拊减为2。武舞曰武功之舞,文舞曰文德之舞,文、武舞生各64名,武舞生各执干、戚,文舞生各执羽籥,另有舞师2人执节引领。

清代沿袭明制,雅乐又称中和韶乐,分祭祀乐、朝会乐、宴乐三种,其中用于祭天的中和韶乐规模最大,兼用文舞、武舞、参与演出的人员也最多,祭天乐章分为九章,分别为"迎神、奠玉帛、进俎、初献、亚献、终献、撤馔、送神、望燎",即按祭天礼仪的九道程序演唱歌舞,歌词表达了对天神的无限歌颂和深切崇仰之情,舞姿则是对歌词的形体解释,并不复杂,八佾即横排8人,

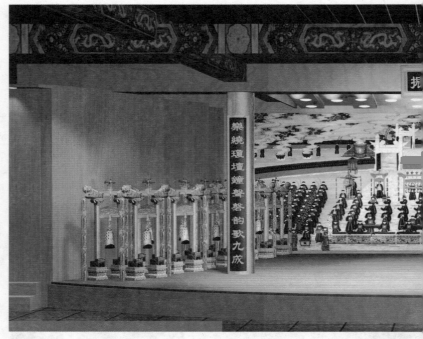

凝禧殿内布景
The Stage Setting of the Hall of Gathered Happines

music was also called Zhongheshaoyue, and divided into sacrificial music, music of conference and music of banquet. The ceremonial music had the largest scale. Both Wen and Wu dances were performed by the largest number of singers and dancers. The music used in heaven worship had nine chapters– greet the god, offer the silk, first offering, second offering, last offering, withdraw the food, send off the god and sacrifice in distance– which were sung according to the nine steps of the ceremony. The songs expressed the limitless praise and profound esteem to the god of heaven. The dancing embodied the song in shape. 64 dancers formed a square group, advanced and retreated in order, creating a grand and spectacular scene.

The nine steps of the ceremonial procedure are in the same process—— the

竖排8人，共64人排列的方阵，进退有序整齐划一，场面隆重壮观。

祭天的九项仪程，都是照此程序：乐生演奏，歌生手执笏版歌唱，舞生舞蹈，由协律郎指挥，鼓乐齐鸣，歌声悠扬，舞姿翩翩，在寒冷的黎明中，给神载歌载舞。

近年来，天坛的研究工作者对祭天乐舞各项资料进行整理，翻查了大量相关明清帝王祭天乐舞的古籍、资料，各类祭祀音乐乐谱、祭祀舞蹈的舞谱、各种古乐器的配器谱等等，从近千万文字资料中初步整理了完整的30多首乐谱。这些古乐的曲谱、节奏等都具有一定的难度，而且其中演奏用的部分乐器，例如排箫、钟、磬、琴、瑟虽然少见，但还有人能够演奏，像建鼓、篪等古乐器已不能够见到，只在天坛还保存并在祭天乐舞馆内展出。

为了进一步让人们在天坛领略到古人"天人合一"的境界，使得逛天坛成为

musicians perform the instruments and the singers hold the scepter while singing. The dancers are dancing while conducted by the official responsible for adjusting the tunes.

In recent years, researchers of the Temple of Heaven have reorganized the documents about the sacrificial music and dancing. They thumb through a number of ancient books and documents about the sacrificial music and dancing in Ming and Qing dynasty, all kinds of books of sacrificial music and dancing; and music books of orchestration ect. They finally work out 30 complete music books from the large amount of written materials. These music books and rhythms are difficult to understand. Some of the musical instruments, such as paixiao, zhong, qing, qin and se, though rarely seen, can still be performed. However, we are unable to have a look at instruments like jiangu and chi, which are only preserved in the Temple of Heaven and exhibited in the Hall for Music and Dancing. In order to allow the tourists to appreciate the sate of "the heaven and man being integrated into a whole" in the Temple of Heaven, and make strolling in it a kind of enjoyment, the Temple of Heaven invest a large sum of money in restoring the Divine Music Office, which will be open to society in the autumn of 2004. In the restored Divine Music Office, besides the professional exhibition rooms of qin, se, di, xiao, yun, songs, music and dancing, the Hall of Gathered Happiness is preserved to perform ancient music. The tourists not only can appreciate the unique exhibition of ancient music, but also the grand scene of performance of ancient music.

The Temple of Heaven embodies rich cultural connotations. There are many touching stories and beautiful legends about the sky in the history. If we truly integrate the historical culture of the Temple of Heaven into the traditional Chinese culture, then the Temple of heaven presented before our eyes is not only an admirable construction, but also an infinite world full of Chinese characteristics and enchantment. The music salvoes accompanied by the drumbeats. The melodious singing and Ceremonial dancing perform

凝禧殿内古乐器陈列——建鼓
An Exhibition of the Ancient Musical Instruments in he Hall
of Gathered Happines—Jiangu

一种享受,天坛投巨资修复了神乐署,并于2004年秋对社会开放。修复后的神乐署除开辟了琴、瑟、鼓、笛、箫、埙、词曲、乐律、舞蹈等专业展室外,还保留着专门用来演奏古乐的凝禧殿,广大游客不仅可以在这里欣赏到独具特色的古乐展览,还可以欣赏规模宏大的古乐演出。

　　天坛有着丰富的文化内涵,历史上的天坛有许多动人的故事和美好的传

our worship to gods at the cold daybreak.

The Temple of Heaven receives thousands of travelers from all over the world every day. Here the fresh air, luxuriantly green grass, prosperous trees, gorgeous flowers, plus the grand Hall of Prayer for Good Harvest and the wonderful Echo Wall may deeply touch the travelers' heart. It looks as if the state of the heaven and man being integrated into a whole was realized in the Temple of Heaven, a beautiful garden.

圆形建筑,方形墙墙,是"天地方圆"的具体体现
The Circular Buildings and Rectangular Walls Represent the Ancient Chinese Thought—"The Heaven Is Round and the Earth Is Square"

说。如果真正把天坛的历史文化融入中国传统文化中,那么展现在人们面前的天坛将不仅是令人赞叹的建筑,更是充满中华神韵和魅力的无穷大世界。

　　每天,天坛要接待成千上万来自世界各地的游客,在这里,空气清新,芳草葱郁,树木繁茂,花儿艳丽,加上祈年殿的雄浑和回音壁的美妙,让人深深感动,仿佛古人所谓"天人合一"的境界,在天坛这座美好园林里实现了。

Ticket

Low Season：November 1st–March 31st

The Ordinary Ticket: 10 Yuan

The Ticket of Scenic Spot: 20 Yuan

One–way Ticket: 30 Yuan

Peak Season：April 1st–October 31st

The Ordinary Ticket: 15 Yuan

The Ticket of Scenic Spot: 20 Yuan

One–way Ticket: 35 Yuan

The Divine Music Office: 10 Yuan

Bus Route

Take Bus No. 106, 20, 120, 803, 36, 17, 7, 742, 729, and get off at the footbridge or the West Gate of the Temple of Heaven

Take Bus No. 106, 34, 35, 36, 6, 707, 734 and get off at the North Gate of the Temple of Heaven

Take Bus No. 34, 35, 36, 6, 39, 39 (branch line), 41, 43, 822 and get off at Fahua Temple (the East Gate of the Temple of Heaven)

Take Bus No. 120, 803, 122 and get off at the South Gate of the Temple of Heaven

The Traveling Route

South Gate—Circular Mound—Imperial Vault of Heaven—Triple Gate——Fasting Palace—Divine Music Office—Danbi Bridge—Long Corridor—Hall of Prayer for Good Harvests—North Gate

East Gate—The Seven–Star Stones—Long Corridor—Hall of Prayer for Good Harvests—Danbi Bridge—Imperial Vault of Heaven—Circular Mound Altar —Fasting Palace—Divine Music Office—West Gate

门　票

淡季:每年11月1日至次年3月31日

　　　普通门票10元

　　　回音壁10元、圜丘坛10元、祈年殿10元、景点票20元,联票30元。

旺季:每年4月1日至10月31日

　　　普通门票15元,景点票20元,联票为35元。

　　　斋宫、神乐署10元

乘车路线

西门:可乘106、20、120、803、36、17、7、729等,快速公交到天桥或天坛西门下车

北门:可乘106、34、35、36、6、707、734等,到天坛北门下车

东门:可乘34、35、36、6、39、39支、41、43、822、地铁5号线等到法华寺下车

南门:可乘120、803、122等到天坛南门下车

游览路线

南门——圜丘坛——皇穹宇——三座门——斋宫——神乐署——丹陛桥——长廊——祈年殿——北门

东门——七星石——长廊——祈年殿——丹陛桥——皇穹宇——圜丘坛——斋宫——神乐署——西门

图书在版编目(CIP)数据

天坛汉英对照/姚安，王桂荃编著.
—北京：北京美术摄影出版社，2008.5
ISBN 978-7-80501-391-6

Ⅰ.天… Ⅱ.①姚… ②王… Ⅲ.天坛—简介—汉、英
Ⅳ. K928.73

中国版本图书馆CIP数据核字(2008)第063702号

天坛
TIAN TAN

姚 安　王桂荃 编著
出版 北京美术摄影出版社
地址 北京北三环中路6号
邮编 100011
网址 www.bph.com.cn
发行 北京出版社出版集团
经销 新华书店
印刷 北京顺诚彩色印刷有限公司
版次 2008年6月第1版第1次印刷
开本 787×1092 1/32
印张 4
书号 ISBN978 -7-80501-391-6/J·347
定价 20.00元
质量监督电话 010-58572393

探科学奥秘
享健康人生
赏艺术瑰宝
品时尚生活

三好书友会——好人·好书·好生活

感谢您购买我们的图书。欢迎您参加我们的三好书友会。在这里，您可以进入我们的北京风光系列《故宫》、《颐和园》，享受皇家园林带来的视觉震撼；可以和您的玩家一起浏览《把玩艺术系列图书》，享受收藏的乐趣；可以关注《奥运之城》、《北京古代建筑精粹》，纵览2008奥运北京的风貌；还可以聆听到《片面之瓷》中收藏带来的故事……

参加方式

非常简单，填写《会员登记表》，邮寄或者传真给我们即可；也可以在我们的网站上下载注册表，填好后发E-mail到我们的注册信箱，成为我们的会员。

会员权利

⊙ 登记以后，将收到会员确认信，成为终身会员
⊙ 不定期收到新书简介
⊙ 有机会成为兼职作者
⊙ 直购图书，将享受免邮费及打折优惠（具体规则见会员确认信）
⊙ 不定期参加各种书友联谊活动

会员义务

⊙ 遵守国家相关法律法规
⊙ 填写的会员资料必须真实有效

三好书友会 邮购方式

邮政地址： 北京市北三环中路6号北京出版社出版集团科学·生活·艺术事业部
邮政编码： 100011
收 款 人： 毛宇楠
E-mail： chgmls@163.com　maoyunan@3hbook.com
网　　址： www.3hbook.com

书友会热线：

（010）-58572512 （010）-58572303 （010）-58572288（传真）
联系人： 陈　刚　毛宇楠

三好书友会——会员登记表

姓名:

性别:

年龄:

通讯地址:

邮编:

E-mail:

电话: 手机:

您购买的图书书名（准确书名）

您在哪一家书店购买的（请写明具体省、市、地区名称）

您对本书的封面设计有什么意见和建议

您是否愿意成为兼职作者（如愿意，请写明专业背景）

您还希望我们出版哪一方面的图书